THE
MULTILINGUAL
TRANSLATOR

Words and Phrases in 15 Languages
to Help You Communicate
With Students of Diverse Backgrounds

Helen H. Moore

S C H O L A S T I C
PROFESSIONAL BOOKS

New York • Toronto • London • Auckland • Sydney

To all new Americans,
immigrants, like me,
and welcome.

Acknowledgments

This book was made possible by the hard work of many people, of many different backgrounds. I'd like to thank all of them, especially:

Terry Cooper, who listened to what I wanted to do, and let me do it; Virginia Dooley, one of the rare ones, a sensitive and sensible editor (and a new friend); Lloyd Chilton, who always said it was a good idea; Nan Mohr, for her encouragement and helpful suggestions; and Jane Lerach, who welcomes and teaches immigrant children every day at JHS 111 in New York's Chinatown.

Logos International, Jaime Lucero, Betty Yuen, Peter Cipkowski, Lana Krhin, Madragor M. Janvier, Sam Kang, Dionisio De La Cruz, Irene Nguyen, Ravi Kotru, Gargi Mukherjee, Kaushal K. Saran, Jamil Daher, James Irani, Maria Tufaro, and CP Language, for their translations; and a special thanks to CP Language for their careful attention to the pronunciation of several of the languages.

All the teachers who advised me, especially: Kit Fung, Amy Hom, Carolyn Dye, Genevieve Grindle, Laura Norton, Steven Sander, Min Hong, Terra Ellingson, Carolyn C. Litke, M. Judy Haynes, Hilarie Susskind, and Marilyn Andre.

And the children whose stories encouraged me: Judy Zeng, Janet Liu, Jerry Ng, David Chan, Julie Ni, Susan Lu, Hui Ying Zhao, Alice Zhou, Jenny Tang, Joanne Huang, Janelle Chin, Thao Le, Su Qin, Chen Liu, Yiki Zhang, Hsuan Li, and Quang Zhang.

Interior design by Vincent Ceci
Cover and interior illustrations by James Graham Hale
Cover design by Vincent Ceci

ISBN 0-590-48923-2

12 11 10 9 8 7 6 5 4 3 2 1   4 5/9
Printed in the U.S.A.

Table of Contents

Introduction

I visited a school in Greenpoint, Brooklyn, in the fall of 1991, where many of the students were recent immigrants from Eastern Europe. One second-grade girl in particular caught my eye. She seemed to have stepped out of television documentary on life in Russia: A round, fair face with serious blue eyes, pursed, doll-like lips, and a charming, anachronistic hairdo, blonde and bobbed, side-parted and pulled across the top of her head, secured there by a huge ribbon bow. I couldn't resist. "Hello," I boomed at her. "What's your name?" To my dismay, the child's eyes brimmed with tears. My "hail fellow, well-met" manner changed, fast, as her teacher pulled me aside and told me: "Flora just arrived from Russia last week. . . she doesn't understand a word of English." Chastened, and somewhat saddened, that day I began a reflective process that would culminate in the publication of the book you're holding now.

As we all know, the first days and weeks of school can be difficult, even when teachers and students share a common language and culture. Every child approaches school with different expectations, abilities, hopes, and fears. Who knows what Flora thought I was saying to her? Clearly, I was making her uncomfortable—maybe she thought I was making some demand she couldn't possibly handle. (Which, in a way, I was.) I know it wasn't my fault, but I'll always feel sorry that my well-intended "Hello" provoked tears instead of a smile. Had I said, "Здравствуйте" (ZDRAH-stvooy-tyeh) instead, who knows?!

I hope this book will help students like Thao Le, a Vietnamese-American child who wrote to me from Rosemead, California, about how things changed in school after he learned English. He wrote, "Now I start the new term everyone in my class is nice, kind, friendly. My classmate, friend, and all the people around me is nice to me. Even if I know much, much, bunch and bunch of English I never forget this and never making fun of people who do not spoke the same language. It really hard to learn English. It really hurt when you left your country. . . ."

Like Thao, many new Americans "really hurt" when they left their native countries under circumstances that can best be described as traumatic—famines, civil wars, deprivation of human rights. We can make the transition easier by greeting them with a few familiar words in their own languages; we might even make our own lives as educators easier. That was my hope in creating this *Multilingual Translator*. I hope that it will make life a little easier and friendlier for students and teachers all over America.

— *Helen H. Moore*

How to Use This Book

As you strive to communicate with your students in this multicultural age, I hope you'll find this book useful. In the traditional "guidebook" sense, of course, it's a quick and easy guide to locate commonly used words and expressions, on the spot, as they're needed.

The fifteen languages included here are the most commonly spoken languages by recent immigrants to the United States according to the United States Immigration and Naturalization Service. These languages were chosen to make the book as useful as possible to the greatest number of teachers and students.

The words and phrases are presented in two ways. For each of the fifteen languages there are four pages of illustrations which are labeled in the language (using authentic alphabets and symbols), phonetically, and in English. The illustrations are child-friendly, and with a quick scan of the page, a word or phrase can be easily found. All of the words and phrases on the illustrations, and additional words and phrases, can also be found in running lists, organized by category, which begin on page 67. Invite foreign-language speaking students to page through the book themselves to find words they want to use. They may find the phrase they want to say and then just point to the picture at first, and you (or a student "buddy") may pronounce the English words.

More Suggestions:
• You may want to reproduce the pages with illustrations and invite students to color them, repeating the words in both languages.
• Your English-speaking students may enjoy learning phrases in different languages.
• You may want to use the reproduced pages in learning centers, or incorporate them into student research projects, homework, or story-starters.
• Challenge students to incorporate the foreign phrases into their writing and speaking.
• Enlarge the illustrations on a copier, and with your own creativity, use as the basis of interactive pocket-charts or bulletin boards.
• When studying countries and cultures, key the languages in the book to the culture being studied.
• Look for connections between English and foreign words. You may encourage a budding etymologist! The possibilities are many!

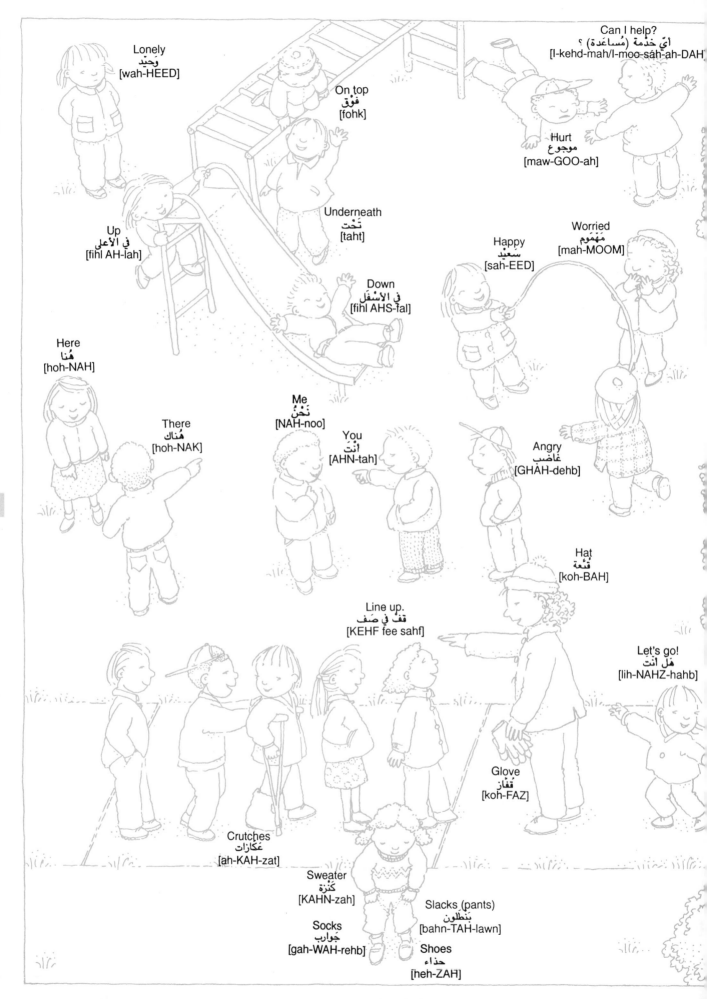

Lonely
وَحيد
[wah-HEED]

On top
فَوْق
[fohk]

Can I help?
أيّ خِدْمة (مُساعَدة) ؟
[I-kehd-mah/I-moo-sáh-ah-DAH]

Hurt
موجوع
[maw-GOO-ah]

Up
في الأعلى
[fihl AH-lah]

Underneath
تَحْت
[taht]

Worried
مَهْموم
[mah-MOOM]

Happy
سَعيد
[sah-EED]

Down
في الأسْفَل
[fihl AHS-fal]

Here
هُنا
[hoh-NAH]

There
هُناك
[hoh-NAK]

Me
نَحْنُ
[NAH-noo]

You
أنْتَ
[AHN-tah]

Angry
غاضِب
[GHAH-dehb]

Hat
قُبَّعة
[koh-BAH]

Line up.
قِف في صَف
[KEHF fee sahf]

Let's go!
هَل أنت
[lih-NAHZ-hahb]

Glove
قُفّاز
[koh-FAZ]

Crutches
عَكّازات
[ah-KAH-zat]

Sweater
كَنْزة
[KAHN-zah]

Slacks (pants)
بَنْطلون
[bahn-TAH-lawn]

Socks
جَوارب
[gah-WAH-rehb]

Shoes
حذاء
[heh-ZAH]

6

Wheelchair
كرسي مُدَوْلَب
[KUR-see MOO-daw-lahb]

Mother
أُم
[uhm]

Father
أب
[ahb]

Principal
مدير
[MOO-dihr]

Brother
أخ
[ahkh]

Office
مكْتَب
[MAHK-tahb]

Sister
أخت
[awkt]

Hello
مَرْحَبا
[mahr-HAH-bah]

Hallway
مَدْخَل (قَاعَة)
[MAHD-kehl]

Thirsty
عَطشان
[AHCH-ahn]

Boys'/Girls' Toilet
حَمَّام الطلاب حَمَّام الطالبات
[hah-MAM ehl-TOHL-lahb/tah-LEE-beht]

Flag
عَلَم
[AH-lahm]

Trash can
سلّة المُهْمَلات
[sahl-LEHT AHL-moh mah-LAT]

Coat
مِعْطَف
[meh-tahf]

Teacher
مُعَلِّم
[moh-AHl-lehm]

Point to...
دل (عَلى)
[dihl (AH-lah)]

Read
إقْرأ !
[ECK-rah]

Raise your hand.
لنَذْهَب !
[ehr-FAH yah-DAHK]

Door
باب
[bab]

Desk
مقْعَد
[MAHK-ahd]

Book
كتاب
[kih-TAHB]

Listen
إسْتَمِعْ !
[ehss-TAH-meh]

Inside
في الدَّاخل
[fih DA-kehl]

Chair
كرْسي
[koor-SEE]

Pen
قلم حبر
[kah-LAHM hehbr]

7

Eyeglasses
نظارات
[nah-ZAH-raht]

Closet
خِزانة
[khah-ZA-nah]

That's better!
هذا أفضل
[HAH-zah ahf-DAHL]

Excuse me.
عَفواً
[ahf-wahn]

Thank you
شُكراً
[SHOOK-rahn]

I need help.
بحاجة إلى مُساعَدة
[beh-HAH-gah ehl-ah MOO-sah-ah-dah]

Stand up.
قِف !
[Kehf]

Pencil
قَلَم رَصاص
[kah-LAHM rah-SAHS]

Good!
جيد
[GAH-yehd]

Tired
تَعبان
[tah-BAN]

Table
طاولة
[TAHW-lah]

Paper
وَرَق
[wah-RAHK]

Shelf
رَف
[rahff]

Can I borrow that?
ممْكِن أسْتعير ذلك ؟
[MOM-kehn ahs-TAH-ehr zah-LEHK]

yes
نعم
[nah-ahm]

Come here.
تَعال هُنا
[tah-AH-lah hoh-NAH]

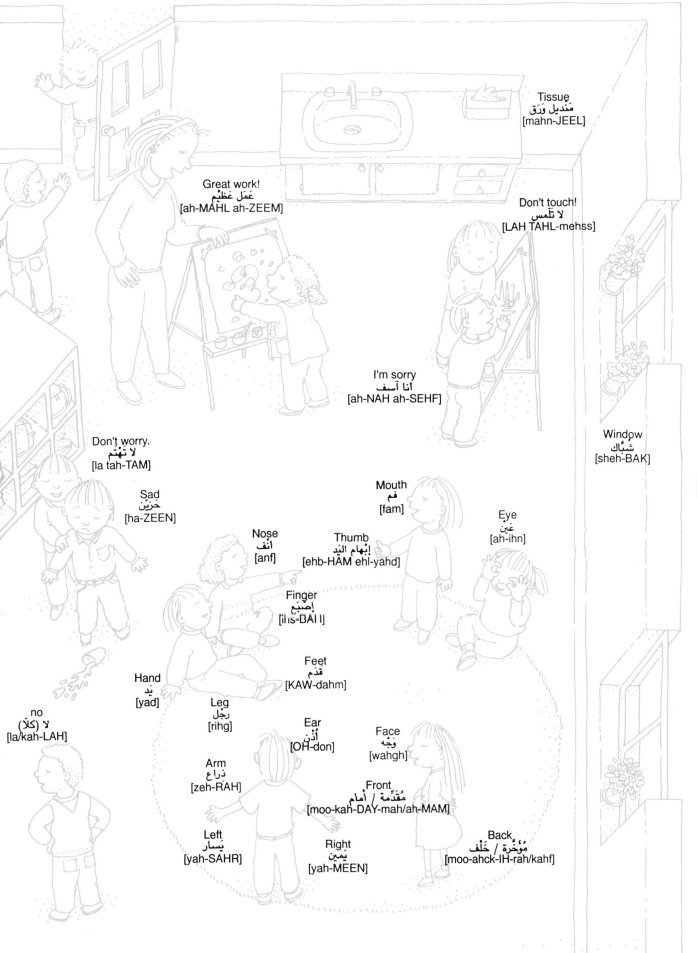

Tissue
مَنديل وَرَق
[mahn-JEEL]

Great work!
عَمَل عَظيم
[ah-MAHL ah-ZEEM]

Don't touch!
لا تَلْمِس
[LAH TAHL-mehss]

I'm sorry
أنا آسِف
[ah-NAH ah-SEHF]

Window
شِبّاك
[sheh-BAK]

Don't worry.
لا تَهْتَم
[la tah-TAM]

Sad
حَزين
[ha-ZEEN]

Mouth
فم
[fam]

Eye
عَين
[ah-ihn]

Nose
أنْف
[anf]

Thumb
إبْهام اليَد
[ehb-HAM ehl-yahd]

Finger
إصْبَع
[ihs-BAH]

Feet
قَدَم
[KAW-dahm]

Hand
يَد
[yad]

Leg
رِجْل
[rihg]

Ear
أُذُن
[OH-don]

Face
وَجْه
[wahgh]

no
لا (كَلّا)
[la/kah-LAH]

Arm
ذِراع
[zeh-RAH]

Front
مُقَدِّمة / أمام
[moo-kah-DAY-mah/ah-MAM]

Left
يَسار
[yah-SAHR]

Right
يَمين
[yah-MEEN]

Back
مُؤَخِّرة / خَلْف
[moo-ahck-IH-rah/kahf]

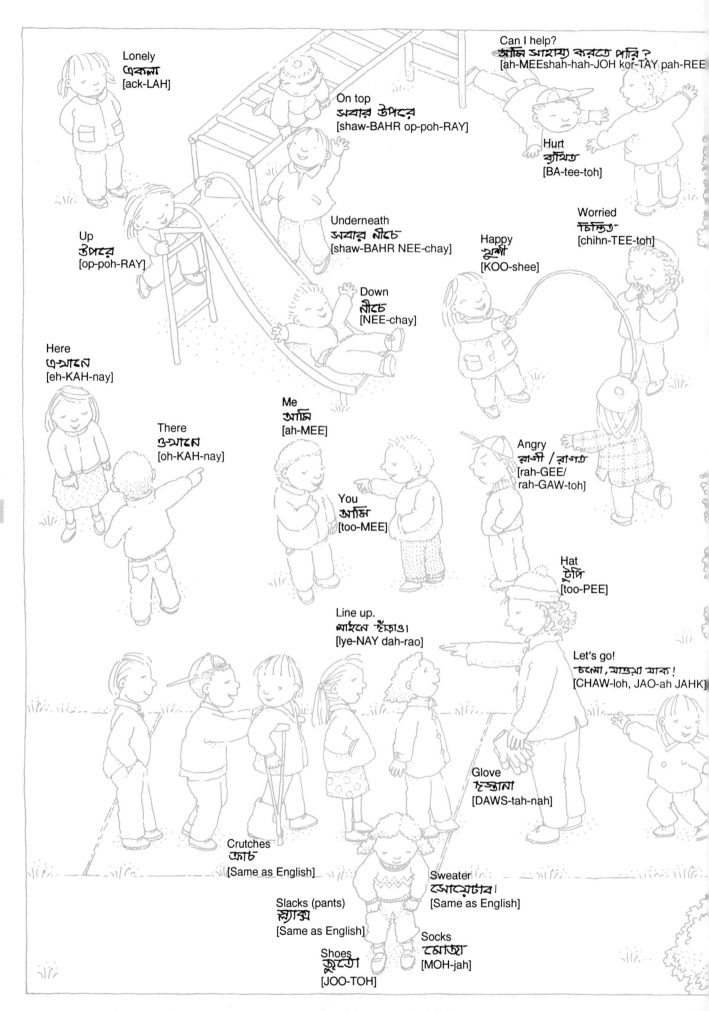

Lonely
একলা
[ack-LAH]

On top
সবার উপরে
[shaw-BAHR op-poh-RAY]

Can I help?
আমি সাহায্য করতে পারি?
[ah-MEEshah-hah-JOH kor-TAY pah-REE]

Hurt
ব্যথিত
[BA-tee-toh]

Underneath
সবার নীচে
[shaw-BAHR NEE-chay]

Worried
চিন্তিত
[chihn-TEE-toh]

Up
উপরে
[op-poh-RAY]

Happy
খুশী
[KOO-shee]

Down
নীচে
[NEE-chay]

Here
এখানে
[eh-KAH-nay]

Me
আমি
[ah-MEE]

There
ওখানে
[oh-KAH-nay]

Angry
রাগী / রাগত
[rah-GEE/rah-GAW-toh]

You
তুমি
[too-MEE]

Hat
টুপি
[too-PEE]

Line up.
লাইনে দাঁড়াও।
[lye-NAY dah-rao]

Let's go!
চলো, যাওয়া যাক!
[CHAW-loh, JAO-ah JAHK]

Glove
দস্তানা
[DAWS-tah-nah]

Crutches
ক্রাচ
[Same as English]

Sweater
সোয়েটার।
[Same as English]

Slacks (pants)
স্ল্যাক্স
[Same as English]

Socks
মোজা
[MOH-jah]

Shoes
জুতো
[JOO-TOH]

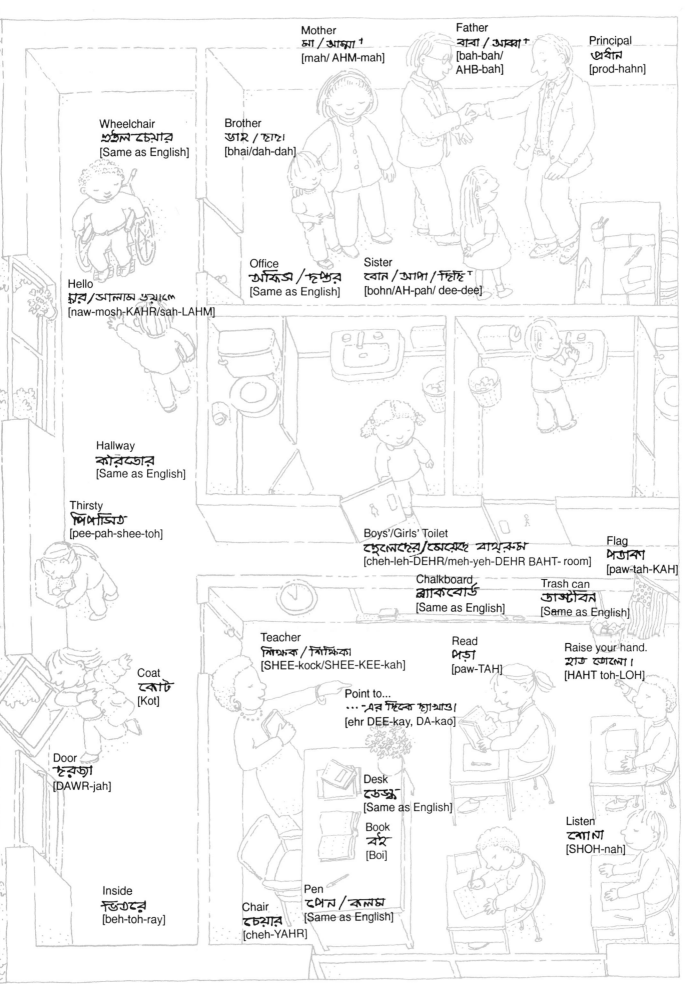

Mother
মা / আম্মা †
[mah/ AHM-mah]

Father
বাবা / আব্বা †
[bah-bah/ AHB-bah]

Principal
প্রধান
[prod-hahn]

Wheelchair
হুইল-চেয়ার
[Same as English]

Brother
ভাই / দাদা
[bhai/dah-dah]

Office
অফিস / দপ্তর
[Same as English]

Sister
বোন / আপা / দিদি †
[bohn/AH-pah/ dee-dee]

Hello
নমস্কার / সালাম আয়কুম
[naw-mosh-KAHR/sah-LAHM]

Hallway
করিডোর
[Same as English]

Thirsty
পিপাসিত
[pee-pah-shee-toh]

Boys'/Girls' Toilet
ছেলেদের/মেয়েদ বাথরুম
[cheh-leh-DEHR/meh-yeh-DEHR BAHT- room]

Flag
পতাকা
[paw-tah-KAH]

Chalkboard
ব্ল্যাকবোর্ড
[Same as English]

Trash can
ডাস্টবিন
[Same as English]

Coat
কোট
[Kot]

Teacher
শিক্ষক / শিক্ষিকা
[SHEE-kock/SHEE-KEE-kah]

Read
পড়া
[paw-TAH]

Raise your hand.
হাত তোলো।
[HAHT toh-LOH]

Point to...
... এর দিকে দ্যাখাও।
[ehr DEE-kay, DA-kao]

Desk
ডেস্ক
[Same as English]

Door
দরজা
[DAWR-jah]

Book
বই
[Boi]

Listen
শোনা
[SHOH-nah]

Inside
ভিতরে
[beh-toh-ray]

Chair
চেয়ার
[cheh-YAHR]

Pen
পেন / কলম
[Same as English]

11

Excuse me.
আপ করো / করুন।
[mahp KAW-roh/mahp koh-RUM]

Eyeglasses
চশমা
[CHAWSH-mah]

Closet
ক্লজেট
[Same as English]

That's better!
এবার ভালো হয়েছে!
[eh-BAHR b-hah-LOH hoh yek-CHEH]

Stand up.
উঠে দাঁড়াও।
[oo-TAY da-RAO]

Thank you
ধন্যবাদ
[DON-noh-bahd]

I need help.
আমার সাহায্য লাগবে
[ah-MAHR shah-hahj-JOH]

Pencil
পেন্সিল
[Same as English]

Good!
ভালো!
[BHAH-loh]

Tired
ক্লান্ত
[KLAHN-toh]

Table
টেবিল
[Same as English]

Paper
কাগজ
[KAH-goj]

Come here.
এখানে এসো!
[eh-KAH-nay eh-SHOH]

Can I borrow that?
আমি কি ওটা ধার করতে পারি?
[akee oh-TAH dhahr kor-teh PAH-ree]

Shelf
তাক
[tahk]

Yes
হ্যাঁ
[hehn]

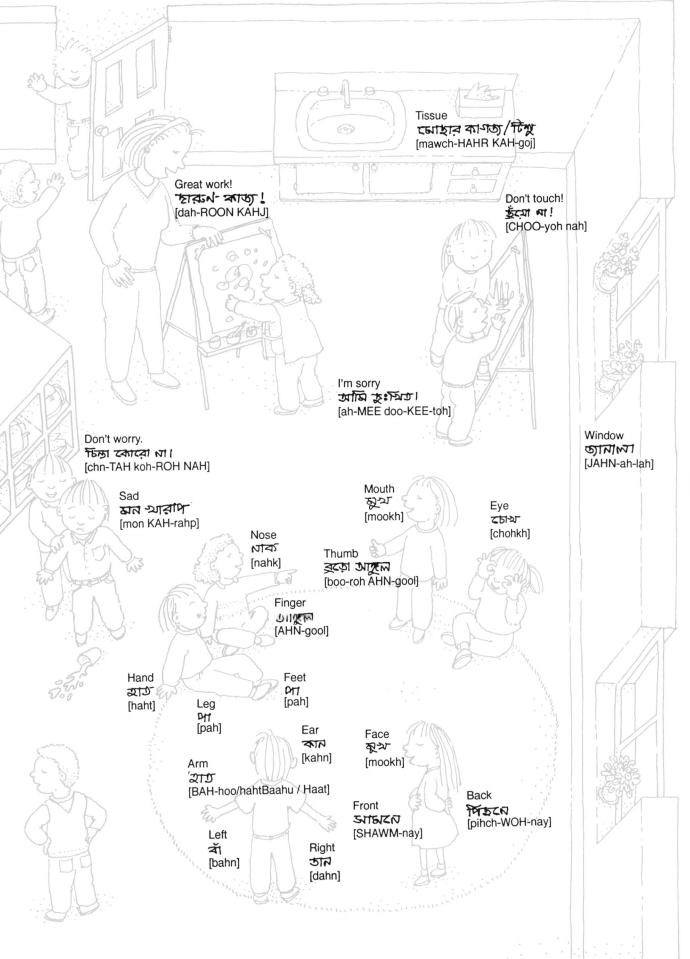

Tissue
মোছার কাগজ/টিস্যু
[mawch-HAHR KAH-goj]

Great work!
হারুন- কাজ !
[dah-ROON KAHJ]

Don't touch!
ছুঁয়ো না !
[CHOO-yoh nah]

I'm sorry
আমি দুঃখিত।
[ah-MEE doo-KEE-toh]

Window
জানালা
[JAHN-ah-lah]

13

Don't worry.
চিন্তা কোরো না।
[chn-TAH koh-ROH NAH]

Sad
মন খারাপ
[mon KAH-rahp]

Mouth
মুখ
[mookh]

Eye
চোখ
[chohkh]

Nose
নাক
[nahk]

Thumb
বুড়ো আঙুল
[boo-roh AHN-gool]

Finger
আঙুল
[AHN-gool]

Hand
হাত
[haht]

Feet
পা
[pah]

Leg
পা
[pah]

Ear
কান
[kahn]

Face
মুখ
[mookh]

Arm
হাত
[BAH-hoo/hahtBaahu / Haat]

Front
সামনে
[SHAWM-nay]

Back
পিছনে
[pihch-WOH-nay]

Left
বাঁ
[bahn]

Right
ডান
[dahn]

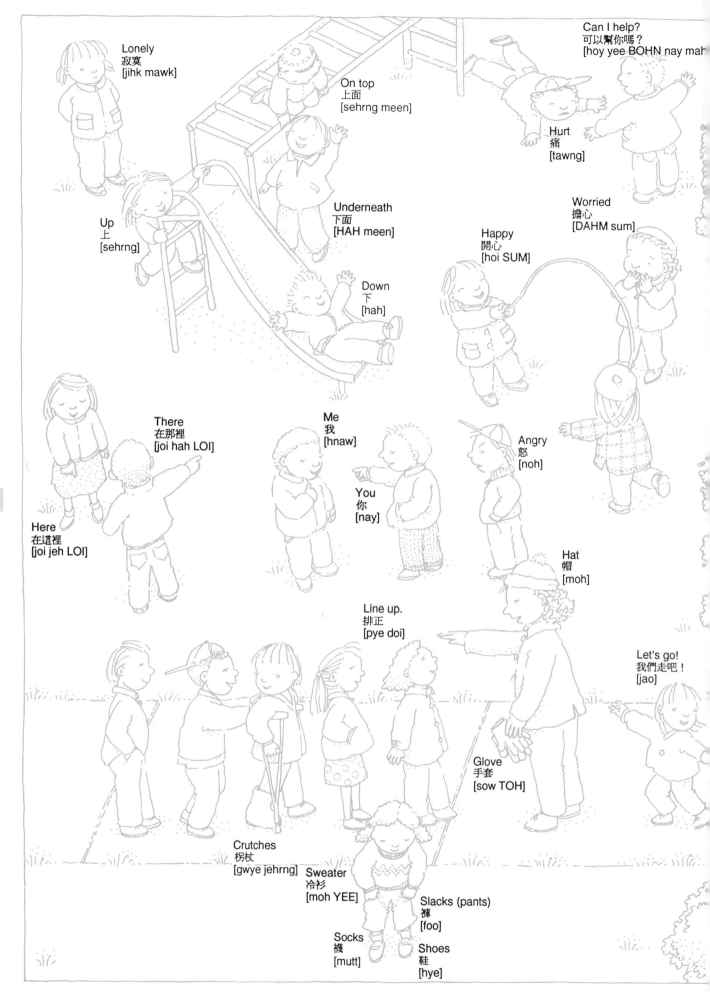

Lonely
寂寞
[jihk mawk]

On top
上面
[sehrng meen]

Can I help?
可以幫你嗎？
[hoy yee BOHN nay mah]

Hurt
痛
[tawng]

Up
上
[sehrng]

Underneath
下面
[HAH meen]

Worried
擔心
[DAHM sum]

Happy
開心
[hoi SUM]

Down
下
[hah]

There
在那裡
[joi hah LOI]

Me
我
[hnaw]

Angry
怒
[noh]

You
你
[nay]

Here
在這裡
[joi jeh LOI]

Hat
帽
[moh]

Line up.
排正
[pye doi]

Let's go!
我們走吧！
[jao]

Glove
手套
[sow TOH]

Crutches
枴杖
[gwye jehrng]

Sweater
冷衫
[moh YEE]

Slacks (pants)
褲
[foo]

Socks
襪
[mutt]

Shoes
鞋
[hye]

14

Wheelchair
輪椅
[run YEE]

Mother
媽媽
[mah mah]

Father
爸爸
[bah BAH]

Principal
校長
[HOW jehrng]

Brother
兄弟
[hihng DAI]

Office
辦公室
[bahn goong SAHT]

Sister
姊姊
[jee moi]

Hello
好嗎
[hoh MAH]

Hallway
走廊
[JAO long]

Thirsty
渴
[hawt]

Boys'/Girls' Toilet
男／女洗手間
[Man/nui sai sau gaan]

Flag
旗
[kay]

Chalkboard
黑板
[hahk BAHN]

Trash can
垃圾
[lye kahp]

Coat
外衣
[hnoi yee]

Teacher
先生
[sihng SAHNG]

Point to...
指向
[jee]

Read
讀
[dawk]

Raise your hand.
舉手
[goi sow]

Desk
書桌
[seh JEE toi]

Book
書
[shoo]

Door
門
[moon]

Listen
聽
[tehng]

Pen
筆
[baht]

Inside
裡面
[LOI MEEN]

Chair
椅
[yee]

15

Excuse me.
原諒我
[yoo-ehn]

Eyeglasses
眼鏡
[hnahn GEHNG]

That's better!
好好多
[hoh dahk DOH]

Closet
衣櫃
[YEE choo]

Thank you
多謝
[DAW jay]

I need help.
我要人幫助
[hnoh SOI yoo bawng joh]

Stand up.
起身
[hay SAHN]

Pencil
鉛筆
[yoo-chn BAHT]

Good!
好
[hoh]

Tired
疲倦
[loi]

Table
餐桌
[toi]

Paper
紙
[JEE]

Shelf
架
[shoo GAH]

Can I borrow that?
我可不可以借用
[Ngoh ho bat ho yi je na goh]

Yes
是
[see]

Come here.
來
[loi]

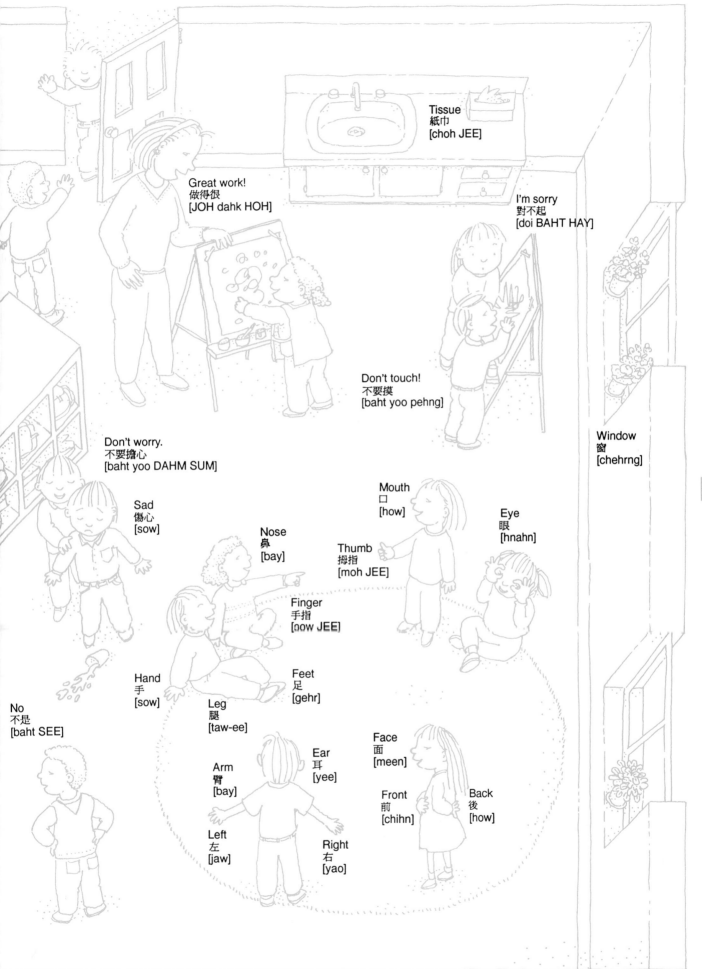

Great work!
做得很
[JOH dahk HOH]

Tissue
紙巾
[choh JEE]

I'm sorry
對不起
[doi BAHT HAY]

Don't touch!
不要摸
[baht yoo pehng]

Window
窗
[chehrng]

17

Don't worry.
不要擔心
[baht yoo DAHM SUM]

Mouth
口
[how]

Eye
眼
[hnahn]

Sad
傷心
[sow]

Nose
鼻
[bay]

Thumb
拇指
[moh JEE]

Finger
手指
[now JEE]

Hand
手
[sow]

Feet
足
[gehr]

Leg
腿
[taw-ee]

No
不是
[baht SEE]

Arm
臂
[bay]

Ear
耳
[yee]

Face
面
[meen]

Left
左
[jaw]

Right
右
[yao]

Front
前
[chihn]

Back
後
[how]

Lonely
تنها
[tan-HAH]

on top
روی
[roo-ee]

Hurt
صدمه دیده
[SAH-dah-may dee-DAY]

Can I help?
من میتوانم کمک بکنم؟
[mee-tah-VAH-nam koh-MAK koh-NAM]

underneath
زیر
[zihr]

up
بالا
[bah-lah]

Worried
نگران
[neh-GAH-rahn]

Happy
شاد
[shod]

down
پایین
[paw-een]

here
اینجا
[ihn-JAH]

me
مرا – بمن
[ma-RAH/beh-MAN]

you
تو – تورا
[toh/toh-RAH]

there
آنجا
[ahn-JAH]

Angry
عصبانی
[a-sah-BAW-nee]

hat
کلاه
[koh-LAH]

Line up.
به صف بایستید
[bh SAHF beh-STEED]

Let's go?
بیا برویم
[beh-RA-veem]

glove
دستکش
[dahst-KEHSH]

crutches
عصا
[ah-SAW]

sweater
جلیقه
[JEH-lih-GAY]

slacks (pants)
شلوار
[shal-VAHR]

socks
جوراب
[joo-RAHB]

shoes
کفش
[kahfsh]

18

wheelchair
ویلچر
[Same as English]

Mother
مادر
[maw-DAHR]

Father
پدر
[peh-DAHR]

Principal
مدیر
[moh-DIHR]

Brother
برادر
[ba-RAH-dahr]

Office
اداره (دفتر)
[en-DAH-reh (dahf-TAHR)]

Sister
خواهر
[khaw-HAHR]

Hello
سلام
[sa-LAHM]

Hallway
راهرو
[rah-roh]

Thirsty
تشنه
[tehsh-NAY]

Boys'/Girls' Toilet
توالت دخترانه – پسرانه
[toh-VAH-leht dohk-TAH-rahm/peh-SAH-rahn]

Flag
پرچم
[pahr-chahm]

Chalkboard
تخته سیاه
[tahk-TEH SEE-aw]

Trash can
آشغالدان
[ahsh-GAHL-dahnn]

coat
کت
[Same as English]

Teacher
معلم
[moh-AH-lehm]

Read
بخوان
[beh-KAHN]

Raise your hand.
دستتان را بلند کنید
[DAHS-teh-tahn-rah boh-LAND koh-need]

Point to...
به .... اشاره کنید
[beh...ESH-ah-RAY koh-NEED]

Door
در
[dahr]

Desk
میز
[meez]

Book
کتاب
[keh-TAHB]

Listen
گوش کن
[GOOSH-kon]

inside
داخل
[DAH-kahl]

Chair
صندلی
[san-dah-LEE]

Pen
قلم
[gah-LAM]

19

eyeglasses
عینک
[AY-nak]

Excuse me.
ببخشید
[beh bahk SHEED]

That's better!
آن بهتر است
[ahn beh-FAHR ahsht]

Closet
کمد
[koh-mohd]

Stand up.
بلند شوید
[boh-LAND shah-VEED]

Thank you
متشکرم
[moh-tah-SHAH-keh-RAM]

I need help.
من به کمک احتیاج دارم
[beh-koh-MAK EH-teh-AHJ dah-ram]

Pencil
مداد
[meh-DOD]

Good!
خوب
[koob]

Tired
خسته
[KAHS-tay]

Table
میز (نیمکت)
[meez(nihm-KAT]

Paper
کاغذ
[kaw-GAZ]

Shelf
قفسه
[gah-FAH-SEH]

Can I borrow that?
آیا من میتوانم آن را قرض کنم؟
[ah-YAH-mee-TAH-vah-NAM ahn-RAH GAHRZ koh-NAM]

Come here.
بیایید اینجا
[ihn-JAH bee-ah-IWD

yes
بله
[ba-LAY]

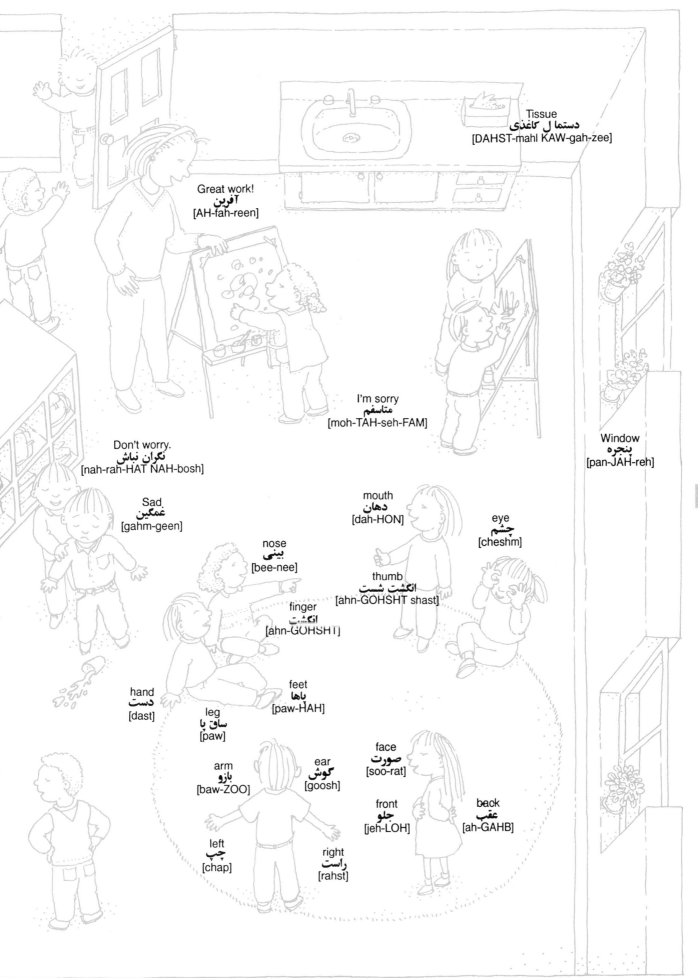

Tissue دستمال کاغذی [DAHST-mahl KAW-gah-zee]

Great work! آفرین [AH-fah-reen]

I'm sorry متاسفم [moh-TAH-seh-FAM]

Don't worry. نگران نباش [nah-rah-HAT NAH-bosh]

Window پنجره [pan-JAH-reh]

21

Sad غمگین [gahm-geen]

mouth دهان [dah-HON]

eye چشم [cheshm]

nose بینی [bee-nee]

thumb انگشت شست [ahn-GOHSHT shast]

finger انگشت [ahn-GOHSHT]

hand دست [dast]

leg ساق پا [paw]

feet پاها [paw-HAH]

arm بازو [baw-ZOO]

ear گوش [goosh]

face صورت [soo-rat]

front جلو [jeh-LOH]

back عقب [ah-GAHB]

left چپ [chap]

right راست [rahst]

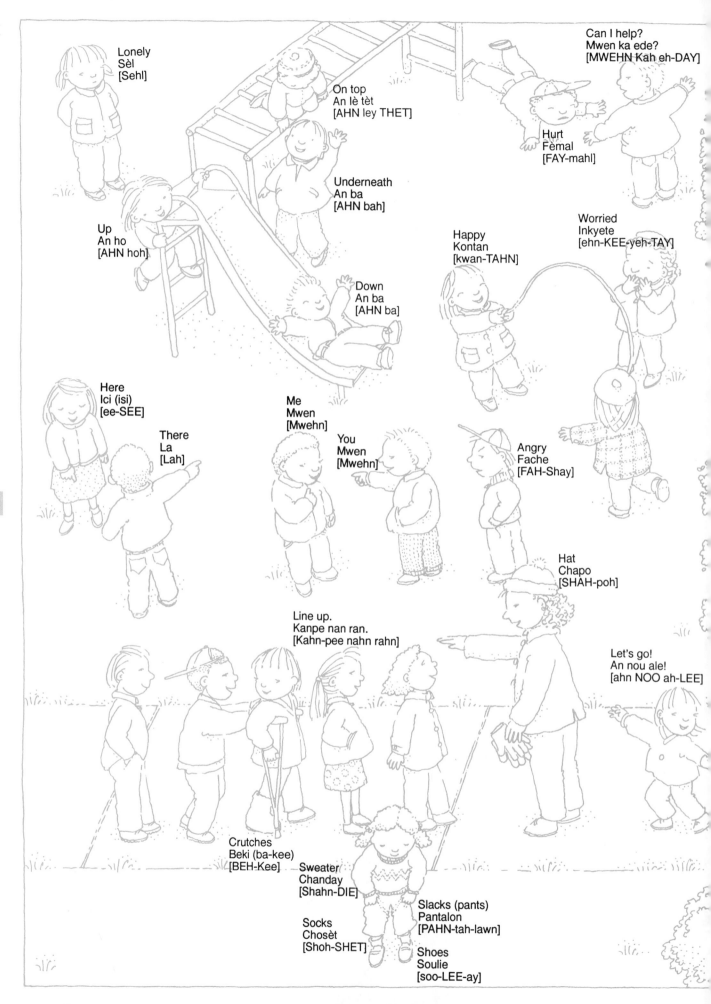

Lonely
Sèl
[Sehl]

On top
An lè tèt
[AHN ley THET]

Can I help?
Mwen ka ede?
[MWEHN Kah eh-DAY]

Hurt
Fèmal
[FAY-mahl]

Underneath
An ba
[AHN bah]

Up
An ho
[AHN hoh]

Worried
Inkyete
[ehn-KEE-yeh-TAY]

Happy
Kontan
[kwan-TAHN]

Down
An ba
[AHN ba]

Here
Ici (isi)
[ee-SEE]

Me
Mwen
[Mwehn]

There
La
[Lah]

You
Mwen
[Mwehn]

Angry
Fache
[FAH-Shay]

Hat
Chapo
[SHAH-poh]

Line up.
Kanpe nan ran.
[Kahn-pee nahn rahn]

Let's go!
An nou ale!
[ahn NOO ah-LEE]

Crutches
Beki (ba-kee)
[BEH-Kee]

Sweater
Chanday
[Shahn-DIE]

Slacks (pants)
Pantalon
[PAHN-tah-lawn]

Socks
Chosèt
[Shoh-SHET]

Shoes
Soulie
[soo-LEE-ay]

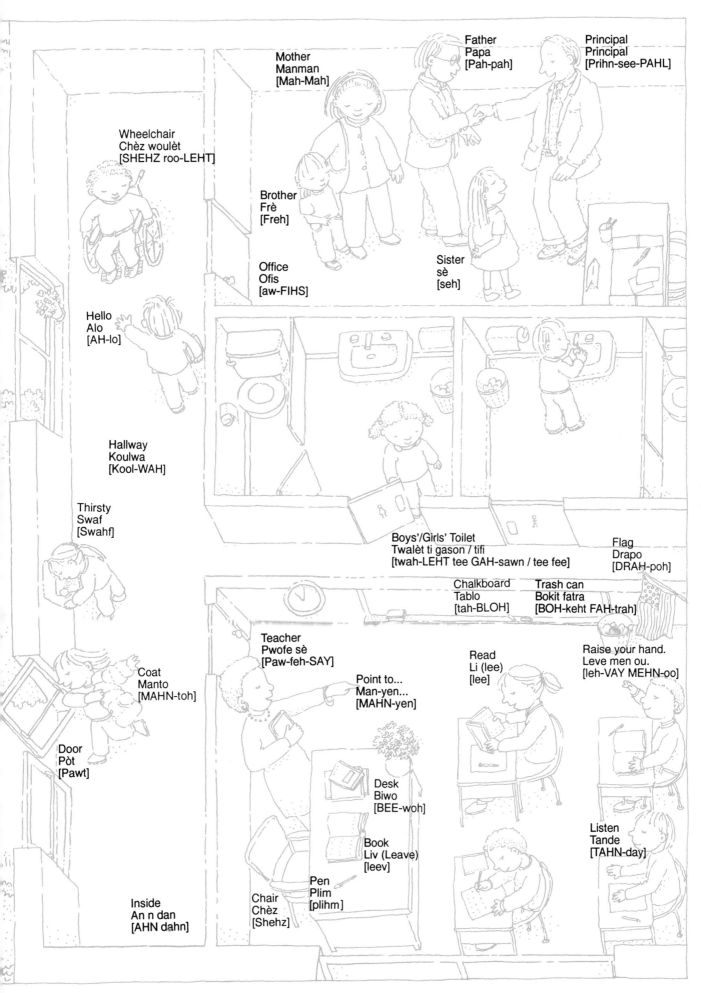

Wheelchair
Chèz woulèt
[SHEHZ roo-LEHT]

Mother
Manman
[Mah-Mah]

Father
Papa
[Pah-pah]

Principal
Principal
[Prihn-see-PAHL]

Brother
Frè
[Freh]

Office
Ofis
[aw-FIHS]

Sister
sè
[seh]

Hello
Alo
[AH-lo]

Hallway
Koulwa
[Kool-WAH]

Thirsty
Swaf
[Swahf]

Boys'/Girls' Toilet
Twalèt ti gason / tifi
[twah-LEHT tee GAH-sawn / tee fee]

Flag
Drapo
[DRAH-poh]

Chalkboard
Tablo
[tah-BLOH]

Trash can
Bokit fatra
[BOH-keht FAH-trah]

Coat
Manto
[MAHN-toh]

Teacher
Pwofe sè
[Paw-feh-SAY]

Point to...
Man-yen...
[MAHN-yen]

Read
Li (lee)
[lee]

Raise your hand.
Leve men ou.
[leh-VAY MEHN-oo]

Door
Pòt
[Pawt]

Desk
Biwo
[BEE-woh]

Book
Liv (Leave)
[leev]

Listen
Tande
[TAHN-day]

Pen
Plim
[plihm]

Inside
An n dan
[AHN dahn]

Chair
Chèz
[Shehz]

23

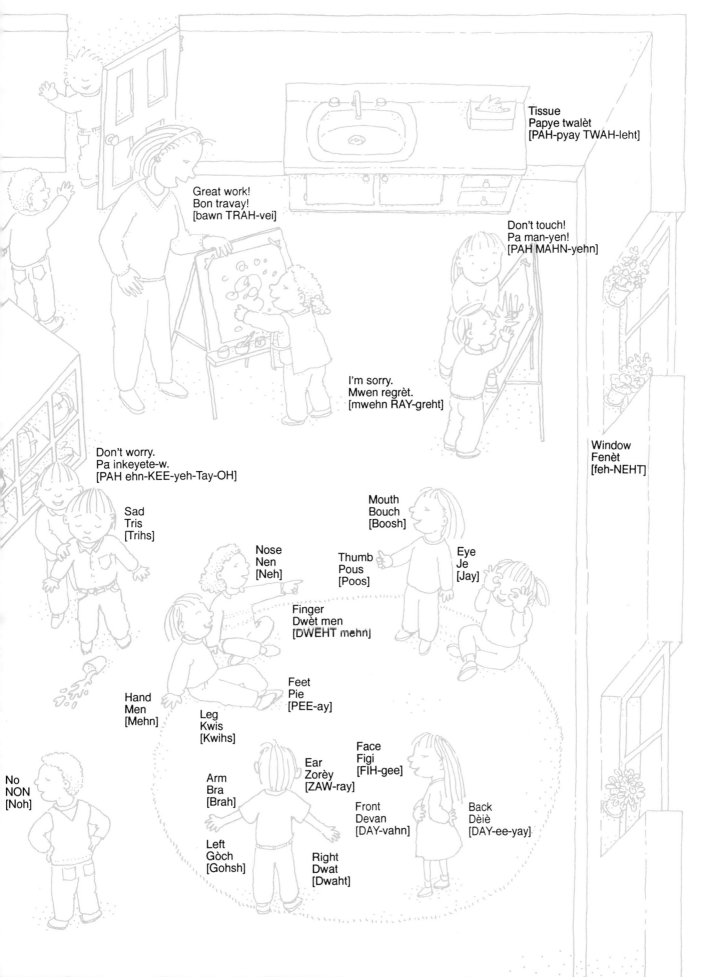

Tissue
Papye twalèt
[PAH-pyay TWAH-leht]

Great work!
Bon travay!
[bawn TRAH-vei]

Don't touch!
Pa man-yen!
[PAH MAHN-yehn]

I'm sorry.
Mwen regrèt.
[mwehn RAY-greht]

Window
Fenèt
[feh-NEHT]

Don't worry.
Pa inkeyete-w.
[PAH ehn-KEE-yeh-Tay-OH]

Sad
Tris
[Trihs]

Mouth
Bouch
[Boosh]

Nose
Nen
[Neh]

Thumb
Pous
[Poos]

Eye
Je
[Jay]

Finger
Dwèt men
[DWEHT mehn]

Hand
Men
[Mehn]

Feet
Pie
[PEE-ay]

Leg
Kwis
[Kwihs]

Face
Figi
[FIH-gee]

No
NON
[Noh]

Arm
Bra
[Brah]

Ear
Zorèy
[ZAW-ray]

Front
Devan
[DAY-vahn]

Back
Dèiè
[DAY-ee-yay]

Left
Gòch
[Gohsh]

Right
Dwat
[Dwaht]

Lonely
अकेला
[AA-kela]

On top
सबसे ऊपर
[Sab-se-OOPer]

Can I help?
क्या मैं मदद कर सकता हूँ ?
[Kya-mane-maddat-kar-SAKTA-whon]

Hurt
चोट
[chot]

underneath
नीचे
[NEE-che]

Up
ऊपर
[OOP-per]

Worried
चिन्तित
[chin-TIT]

Happy
खुश
[khuush]

Down
नीचे
[NEE-che]

here
यहाँ
[YA-ha]

there
वहाँ
[Vah-HA]

Me
मुझे
[MU-jhe]

You
तुम
[TU-m]

Angry
गुस्सा
[Gus-sa]

Hat
हैट
[HAT]

Line up.
कतार में खड़े हो
[KATAR may kha-re ho]

Let's go?
चलो चलें
[CHE -lo CHA -len]

Glove
दस्ताना
[das-taNAA]

Crutches
वैशाखी
[way-SHA-key]

Sweater
स्वेटर
[Sweater]

Slacks (pants)
पतलून
[Pat-LOON]

Socks
मोजा
[MO-ja]

Shoes
जूता
[JU-ta]

Wheelchair
व्हील चेयर
[Wheelchair]

Mother
माता
[MA-ta]

Father
पिता
[PEE-ta]

Principal
प्राचार्य
[PRA-char-ya]

Brother
भाई
[b-hai]

Office
औफिस
[Office]

Sister
बहन
[BA-HAN]

Hello
नमस्ते
[Hello]

Hallway
बरामदा
[VáRANda]

Thirsty
प्यासा
[Pya-asa]

Boys'/Girls' Toilet
स्त्री / पुरूष शौचालय
[Sauch-cha-lay-IS-tree/Pu-roos]

Flag
झंडा
[JHAN-da]

Chalkboard
ब्लैकबोर्ड
[Black board]

Trash can
कूड़ादान
[KOO-RA dhan]

Teacher
शिक्षक
[SHIKCHHAK]

Point to...
इशारा करो
[EE-shara karo]

Read
पढ़ना
[Pad-ho]

Raise your hand.
हाथ उठाओ
[HAAT-uthao]

Coat
कोट
[Coat]

Door
दरवाजा
[dar-WA-ja]

Desk
मेज
[maize]

Book
किताब
[KEE-TAB]

Listen
सुनो
[Soo-no]

Pen
कलम
[KA-lam]

inside
अन्दर
[AAN-dar]

Chair
कुर्सी
[Kur-shee]

27

Excuse me.
मुझे क्षमा करो
[Muje Ksháma karo]

Eyeglasses
चश्मा
[shash-MAA]

That's better!
वह अच्छा है
[wha A-ccha hay]

Closet
आलमारी
[AAL-maree]

Stand up.
उठो
[OOT-ho]

Thank you
शुक्रिया धन्यवाद
[Shu-kriya Dhan-ya-baad]

I needhelp.
मुझे मदद चाहिये
[MU-je madad CHA-EY]

Pencil
पैन्सिल
[Pencil]

Good!
अच्छा
[A-cha]

Tired
थका
[Tha-ka]

Table
मेज़
[maize]

Paper
कागज
[KA-gaj]

Shelf
पटरी
[PAAT-RE]

Can I borrow that?
क्या मैं वह ले सकता हूँ ?
[KYA MAIN WAH LE SAKTA HUN?]

Yes
हाँ
[Hah]

Come here.
यहाँ आओ
[YAh-ha AO]

28

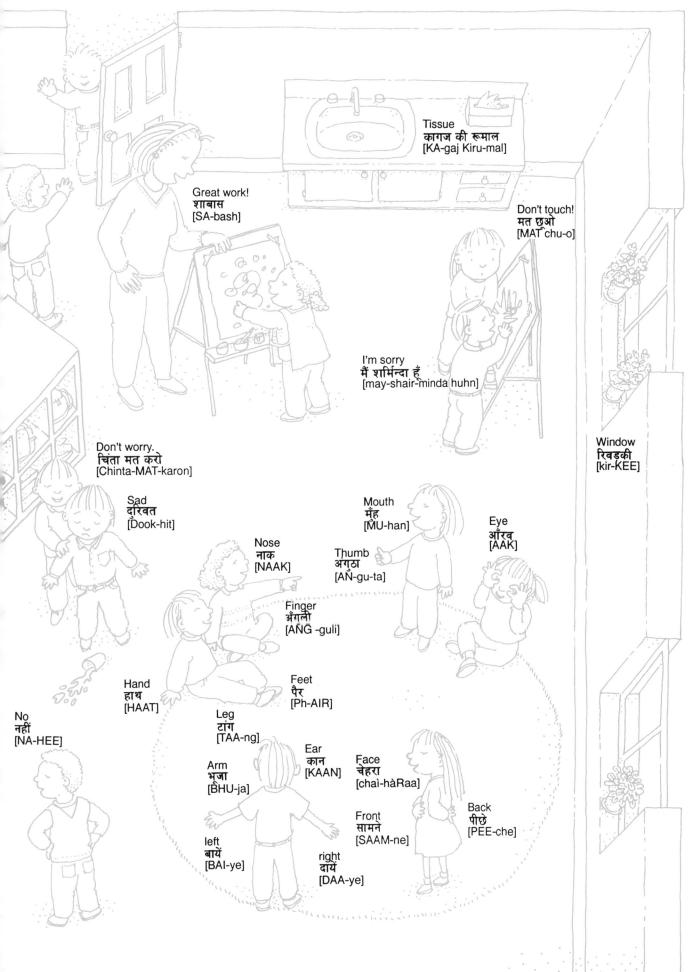

Tissue
कागज की रूमाल
[KA-gaj Kiru-mal]

Great work!
शाबास
[SA-bash]

Don't touch!
मत छुओ
[MAT chu-o]

I'm sorry
मैं शर्मिन्दा हूँ
[may-shair-minda huhn]

Window
रिवड़की
[kir-KEE]

Don't worry.
चिंता मत करो
[Chinta-MAT-karon]

Sad
दुखित
[Dook-hit]

Mouth
मुँह
[MU-han]

Eye
आँख
[AAK]

Nose
नाक
[NAAK]

Thumb
अगूठा
[AN-gu-ta]

Finger
अँगुली
[ANG -guli]

Hand
हाथ
[HAAT]

Feet
पैर
[Ph-AIR]

Leg
टांग
[TAA-ng]

No
नहीं
[NA-HEE]

Arm
भुजा
[BHU-ja]

Ear
कान
[KAAN]

Face
चेहरा
[chai-hàRaa]

Front
सामने
[SAAM-ne]

Back
पीछे
[PEE-che]

left
बायें
[BAI-ye]

right
दायें
[DAA-ye]

29

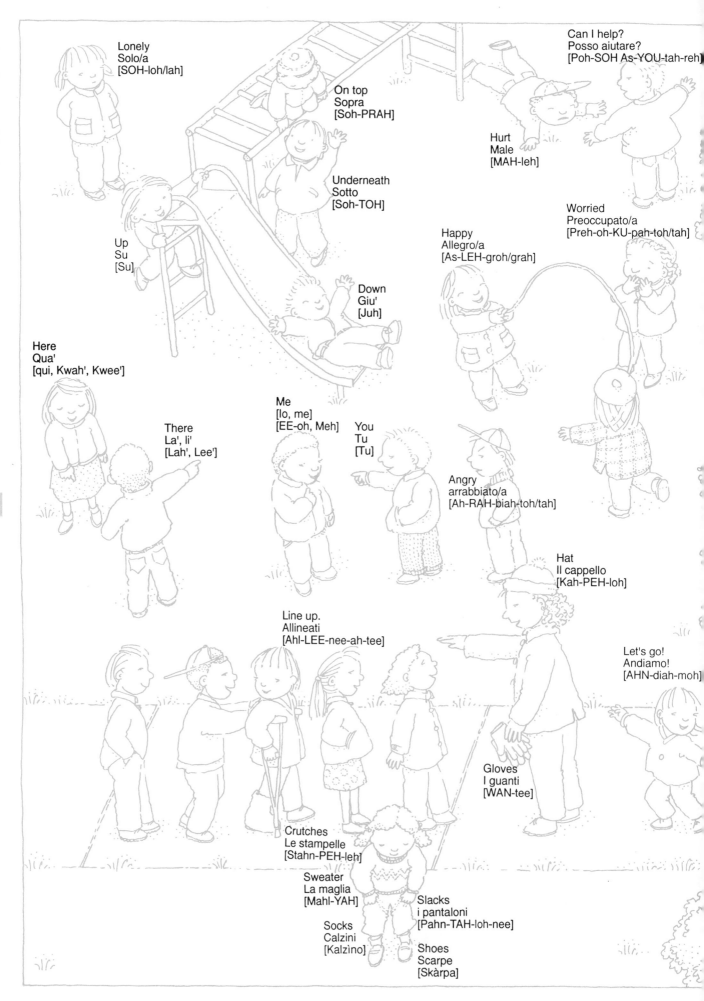

Lonely
Solo/a
[SOH-loh/lah]

On top
Sopra
[Soh-PRAH]

Underneath
Sotto
[Soh-TOH]

Up
Su
[Su]

Down
Giu'
[Juh]

Here
Qua'
[qui, Kwah', Kwee']

There
La', li'
[Lah', Lee']

Me
[Io, me]
[EE-oh, Meh]

You
Tu
[Tu]

Angry
arrabbiato/a
[Ah-RAH-biah-toh/tah]

Can I help?
Posso aiutare?
[Poh-SOH As-YOU-tah-reh]

Hurt
Male
[MAH-leh]

Worried
Preoccupato/a
[Preh-oh-KU-pah-toh/tah]

Happy
Allegro/a
[As-LEH-groh/grah]

Hat
Il cappello
[Kah-PEH-loh]

Let's go!
Andiamo!
[AHN-diah-moh]

Line up.
Allineati
[Ahl-LEE-nee-ah-tee]

Gloves
I guanti
[WAN-tee]

Crutches
Le stampelle
[Stahn-PEH-leh]

Sweater
La maglia
[Mahl-YAH]

Slacks
i pantaloni
[Pahn-TAH-loh-nee]

Socks
Calzini
[Kalzìno]

Shoes
Scarpe
[Skàrpa]

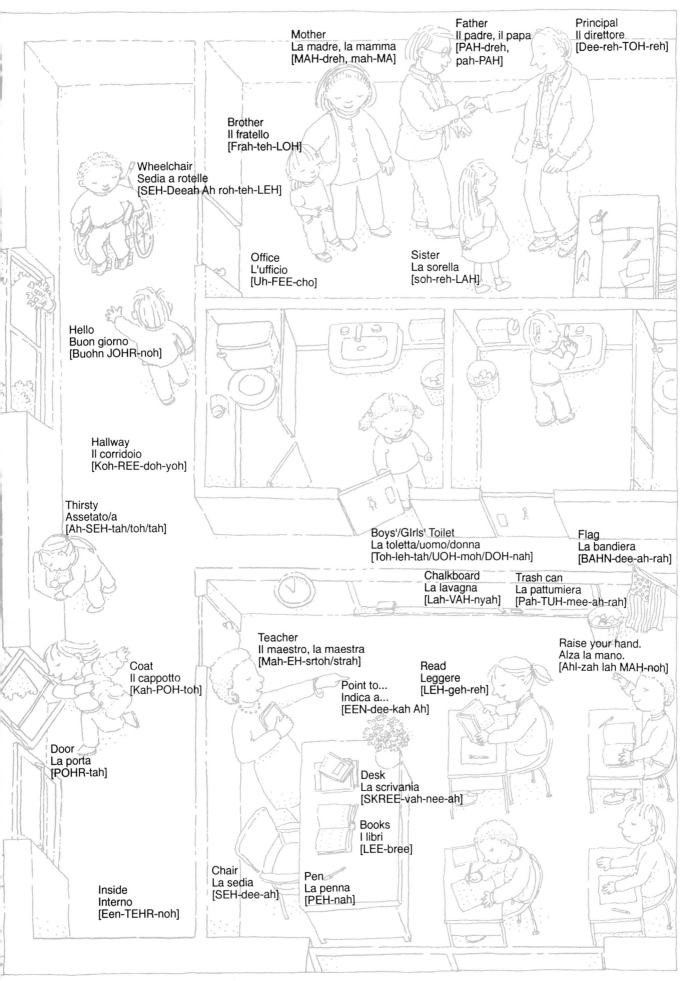

Mother
La madre, la mamma
[MAH-dreh, mah-MA]

Father
Il padre, il papa
[PAH-dreh, pah-PAH]

Principal
Il direttore
[Dee-reh-TOH-reh]

Brother
Il fratello
[Frah-teh-LOH]

Wheelchair
Sedia a rotelle
[SEH-Deeah Ah roh-teh-LEH]

Office
L'ufficio
[Uh-FEE-cho]

Sister
La sorella
[soh-reh-LAH]

Hello
Buon giorno
[Buohn JOHR-noh]

Hallway
Il corridoio
[Koh-REE-doh-yoh]

Thirsty
Assetato/a
[Ah-SEH-tah/toh/tah]

Boys'/Girls' Toilet
La toletta/uomo/donna
[Toh-leh-tah/UOH-moh/DOH-nah]

Flag
La bandiera
[BAHN-dee-ah-rah]

Chalkboard
La lavagna
[Lah-VAH-nyah]

Trash can
La pattumiera
[Pah-TUH-mee-ah-rah]

Coat
Il cappotto
[Kah-POH-toh]

Teacher
Il maestro, la maestra
[Mah-EH-srtoh/strah]

Point to...
Indica a...
[EEN-dee-kah Ah]

Read
Leggere
[LEH-geh-reh]

Raise your hand.
Alza la mano.
[Ahl-zah lah MAH-noh]

Door
La porta
[POHR-tah]

Desk
La scrivania
[SKREE-vah-nee-ah]

Books
I libri
[LEE-bree]

Chair
La sedia
[SEH-dee-ah]

Pen
La penna
[PEH-nah]

Inside
Interno
[Een-TEHR-noh]

32

Excuse me.
Scusami
[SKUH-sah-mee]

Eyeglasses
Gli occhiali
[Oh-KIAH-lee]

That's better!
Molto meglio!
[MOL-toh Meh-glioh]

Closet
Il guardaroba
[WHAR-dah roh-bah]

Thank you
Grazie
[GRAH-zyeah]

I need help.
Ho bisogno d'aiuto.
[Oh bee-SOH-nyoh
dah' Ah-EEYOU-toh]

Stand up.
Alzati
[Ahl-ZAH-tee]

Pencil
La matita
[MAH-tee-tah]

Good!
Bene!
[BEH-neh]

Tired
Stanco/a
[STAHN-koh/kah]

Table
Il tavolo
[TAH-voh-loh]

Paper
La carta
[KAR-tah]

Shelf
I scaffali
[Skah-FAH-lee]

Can I borrow that?
Me lo presti?
[Mee loh PREH-sti]

Yes
Si'
[See']

Come here.
Vieni qua
[VIEH-nee kwah]

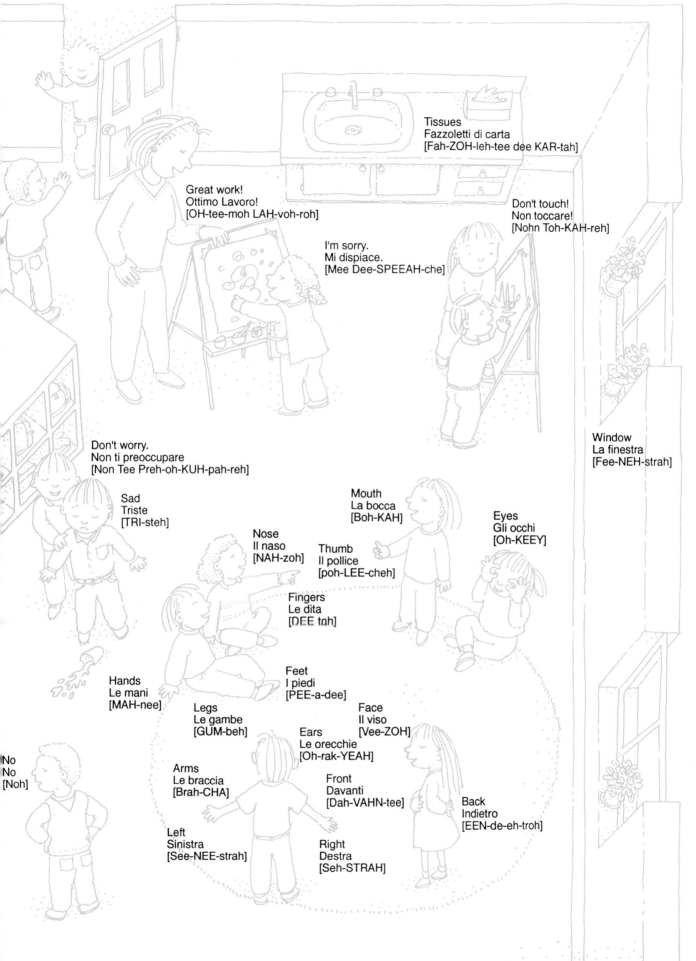

Tissues
Fazzoletti di carta
[Fah-ZOH-leh-tee dee KAR-tah]

Great work!
Ottimo Lavoro!
[OH-tee-moh LAH-voh-roh]

Don't touch!
Non toccare!
[Nohn Toh-KAH-reh]

I'm sorry.
Mi dispiace.
[Mee Dee-SPEEAH-che]

Window
La finestra
[Fee-NEH-strah]

Don't worry.
Non ti preoccupare
[Non Tee Preh-oh-KUH-pah-reh]

Mouth
La bocca
[Boh-KAH]

Eyes
Gli occhi
[Oh-KEEY]

Sad
Triste
[TRI-steh]

Nose
Il naso
[NAH-zoh]

Thumb
Il pollice
[poh-LEE-cheh]

Fingers
Le dita
[DEE tah]

Hands
Le mani
[MAH-nee]

Feet
I piedi
[PEE-a-dee]

Legs
Le gambe
[GUM-beh]

Face
Il viso
[Vee-ZOH]

Ears
Le orecchie
[Oh-rak-YEAH]

No
No
[Noh]

Arms
Le braccia
[Brah-CHA]

Front
Davanti
[Dah-VAHN-tee]

Back
Indietro
[EEN-de-eh-troh]

Left
Sinistra
[See-NEE-strah]

Right
Destra
[Seh-STRAH]

Lonely
외로운
(Wei roh woon)

On top
꼭떼기
(Kkok Ddeh gi)

Can I help?
도와 드릴까요?
(Doh wah due ril kkah yo?)

Hurt
아픈
(Ah poon)

Underneath
밑
(Mit)

Worried
걱정된
(Kohk chong dwen)

Happy
행복한
(Hang bohk hahn)

Up
위
(Ui)

Down
아리
(Ah rae)

Here
여기
(Yoh gi)

Me
나에게
(Nah eh keh)

You
당신
(Dahng shin)

Angry
화난
(Hwa nahn)

There
저기
(Joh gi)

Hat
모자
(Moh jah)

Let's go!
갑시다!
(Kab shi tah)

Line up.
줄 서십시요.
(Jool soh shib si yo)

Glove
장갑
(Chang gahb)

Crutches
목다리
(Moh dah rih)

Sweater
스웨터
(Sweater)

Slacks(pants)
바지
(Bah ji)

Socks
양말
(Yang Mahl)

Shoes
신발
(Shin bahl)

Wheelchair
휠체어
(Wheel chair)

Mother
어머니
(Uh muh nih)

Brother
형제
(Hyung jae)

Father
아버지
(Ah buh ji)

Principal
교장
(Kyo jahng)

Office
사무실
(Sah moo shil)

Sister
자매
(Cha mah)

Hello
여보세요
(Yuh boh seh yo)

Hallway
복도
(Bok doh)

Boys'/girls' toilet
남자용 화장실; 여자용 화장실
(Nahm jah yong hwa chang shil)
(Yuh jah yong hwa chang shil)

Flag
국기
(Kook kih)

Thirsty
목마른
(Mohk mah reun)

Chalkboard
칠판
(Chil pahn)

Trash can
쓰레기 통
(Sseu reh ki tong)

Teacher
선생
(Suhn sang)

Point to ...(blank)
...지적하라
(...chi joh hah rah)

Read
읽다
(Eel tah)

Raise your hand.
손을 드세요.
(Sohn eul deu seh yo)

Coat
코트
(coat)

Desk
책상
(Chak sahng)

Door
문
(Moon)

Book
책
(Chak)

Listen
듣다
(Deut tah)

Chair
의자
(Ui cha)

Pen
펜
(Pen)

Inside
내부
(Nah boo)

35

Excuse me.
실례합니다.
(Shil lyeh hahm ni tah)

Eyeglasses
안경
(Ahn kyong)

That's better!
그 것이 더 좋다!
(Geu got ee doh chot tah)

Closet
옷장
(Oht chang)

Stand up.
일어 서십시오.
(Il oh soh shib si yo)

Thank you
감사합니다
(Kam sah hahm ni tah)

I need help.
도와 주십시오.
(Do wha joo sip sih yo)

Pencil
연필
(Yun pil)

Good!
좋다!
(Chot tah!)

Tired
피곤한
(Pi gohn hahn)

Table
상
(Sahng)

Paper
종이
(Chong ee)

Shelf
선반
(Suhn bahn)

Can I borrow that?
그 것을 빌릴 수 있을까요?
(Kue goht eul bil lil soo it sseul kkah yo?)

Yes
네
(Nyeh)

Come here.
이리 오십시오.
(Ee ri oh shib si yo)

Tissue
화장지
(Hwa chang chi)

Great work!
잘했어!
(Chol hat suh!)

Don't touch!
만지지 마세요
(Mahn chi chi mah seh yo)

I'm sorry.
미안 합니다.
(Mi ahn ham ni tah)

Don't worry.
걱정하지 마세요.
(Kok jung hah ji ma seh yo)

Window
창문
(Chang moon)

Sad
슬픈
(Seul poon)

Mouth
입
(Ip)

Nose
코
(Koh)

Thumb
엄지 손가락
(Uhm ji sohn
gah rahk)

Eye
눈
(Noon)

Finger
손가락
(Sohn gah rahk)

Feet
발
(Bahl)

Hand
손
(Sohn)

Leg
다리
(Dah ri)

No
아니요
(Ah ni yo)

Ear
귀
(Kui)

Face
얼굴
(Uhl gool)

Arm
팔
(Pahl)

Front
앞
(Ahp)

Back
뒤
(Dui)

Left
왼쪽
(When jjok)

Right
오른쪽
(Oh reun jjok)

Lonely
samotny
[sahm-MOTT-neh]

On top
na górze   na
[GOR-sheh]

Can I help?
Ja ci pomegę?
[yah chee poh-MEH-geh]

Hurt
uderzony
[oo-deh-ZHOH-neh]

Worried
zdenerowany
[zoh-leh-neh-roh-VAH-neh]

Up
góra
[GOH-rah]

Underneath
pod spodem
[pohd SPUH-dem]

Happy
szczęśliwy
[shcheh-SHLEE-veh]

Down
dole
[DOH-leh]

Here
tu
[too]

There
tam
[tahm]

Me
Mnie
[mnyeh]

You
Ty
[teh]

Angry
zły
[zweh]

Hat
kapelusz
[kha-PEL-oosh]

Line up.
Stań w szeregu.
[stahn veh sheh-REH-goo]

Glove
ręckawiczki
[re-kav-EETCH-kee]

Crutches
kule inwalidzkie
[kooh-LEH in-vah-LEEDTZ-kee]

Sweater
sweter
[SVER-tehr]

Slacks (pants)
spodnie
[SPOD-nyeh]

Socks
skarpety
[skar-PHE-teh]

Shoes
buty
[BOO-teh]

38

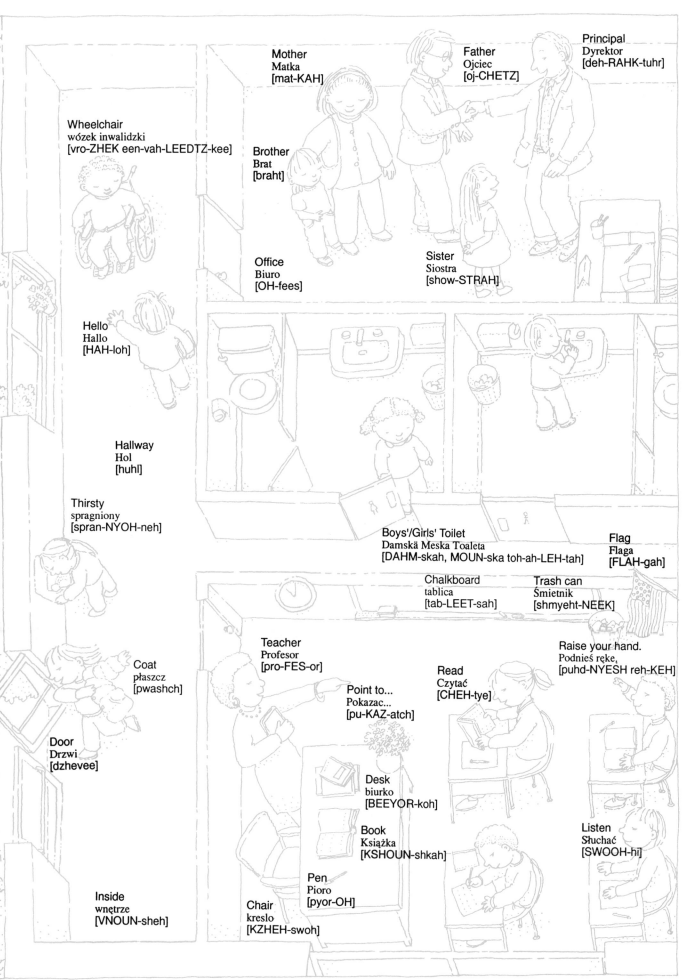

Wheelchair
wózek inwalidzki
[vro-ZHEK een-vah-LEEDTZ-kee]

Mother
Matka
[mat-KAH]

Brother
Brat
[braht]

Father
Ojciec
[oj-CHETZ]

Principal
Dyrektor
[deh-RAHK-tuhr]

Office
Biuro
[OH-fees]

Sister
Siostra
[show-STRAH]

Hello
Hallo
[HAH-loh]

Hallway
Hol
[huhl]

Thirsty
spragniony
[spran-NYOH-neh]

Boys'/Girls' Toilet
Damskä Meska Toaleta
[DAHM-skah, MOUN-ska toh-ah-LEH-tah]

Flag
Flaga
[FLAH-gah]

Chalkboard
tablica
[tab-LEET-sah]

Trash can
Śmietnik
[shmyeht-NEEK]

Coat
płaszcz
[pwashch]

Teacher
Profesor
[pro-FES-or]

Point to...
Pokazac...
[pu-KAZ-atch]

Read
Czytać
[CHEH-tye]

Raise your hand.
Podnieś rękę,
[puhd-NYESH reh-KEH]

Door
Drzwi
[dzhevee]

Desk
biurko
[BEEYOR-koh]

Book
Książka
[KSHOUN-shkah]

Listen
Słuchać
[SWOOH-hi]

Pen
Pioro
[pyor-OH]

Inside
wnętrze
[VNOUN-sheh]

Chair
kreslo
[KZHEH-swoh]

Eyeglasses
okulary
[oh-koo-LAH-reh]

That's better!
To jest lepsze!
[toh yest LEP-sheh]

Closet
Szafa
[SHAH-fah]

Excuse me.
Przepraszam.
[psheh-PRAH-sham]

Thank you
Dziekuję
[gin-KOO-yeh]

I need help.
Pomóż mi.
[Poh-MUHTS mee]

Stand up.
Wstań.
[vstahn]

Pencil
Olowek
[oh-WOH-vek]

Good!
Dobry!
[DOH-breh]

Tired
zmęczony
[zmoun-CHOH-neh]

Table
stół
[stoow]

Paper
Papier
[pah-PEE-yer]

Shelf
Półka
[poow-KAH]

Can I borrow that?
Ja ci pożyczę?
[yah cee poz-SHECH-eh]

Come here.
Chodz tu.
[hutch too]

Yes
Tak
[tahk]

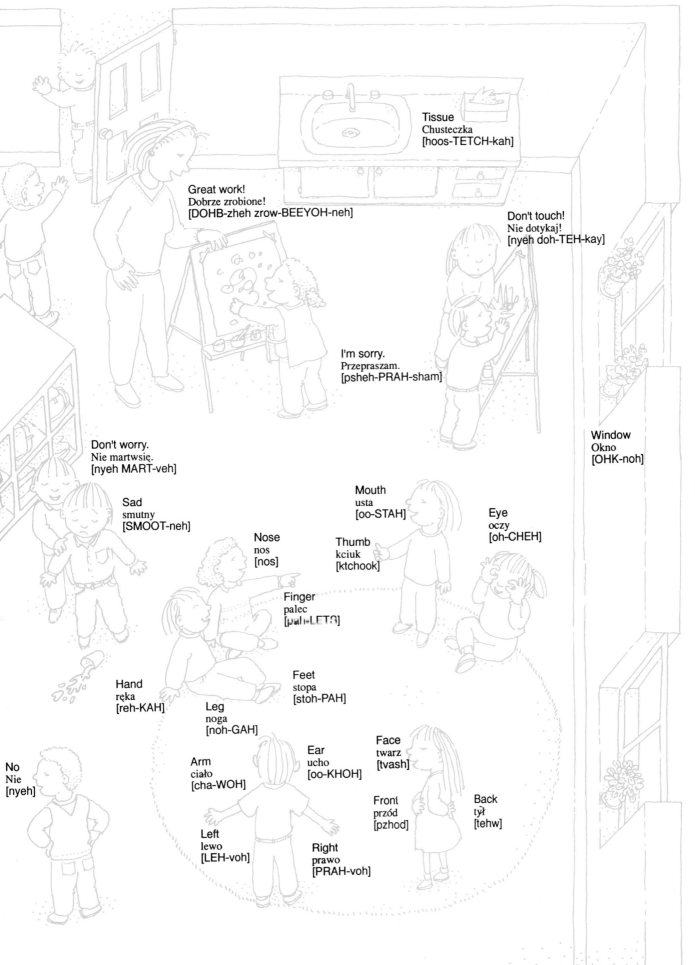

Tissue
Chusteczka
[hoos-TETCH-kah]

Great work!
Dobrze zrobione!
[DOHB-zheh zrow-BEEYOH-neh]

Don't touch!
Nie dotykaj!
[nyeh doh-TEH-kay]

I'm sorry.
Przepraszam.
[psheh-PRAH-sham]

Window
Okno
[OHK-noh]

Don't worry.
Nie martwsię.
[nyeh MART-veh]

Sad
smutny
[SMOOT-neh]

Mouth
usta
[oo-STAH]

Eye
oczy
[oh-CHEH]

Nose
nos
[nos]

Thumb
kciuk
[ktchook]

Finger
palec
[pah-LETS]

Feet
stopa
[stoh-PAH]

Hand
ręka
[reh-KAH]

Leg
noga
[noh-GAH]

Face
twarz
[tvash]

Arm
ciało
[cha-WOH]

Ear
ucho
[oo-KHOH]

No
Nie
[nyeh]

Front
przód
[pzhod]

Back
tył
[tehw]

Left
lewo
[LEH-voh]

Right
prawo
[PRAH-voh]

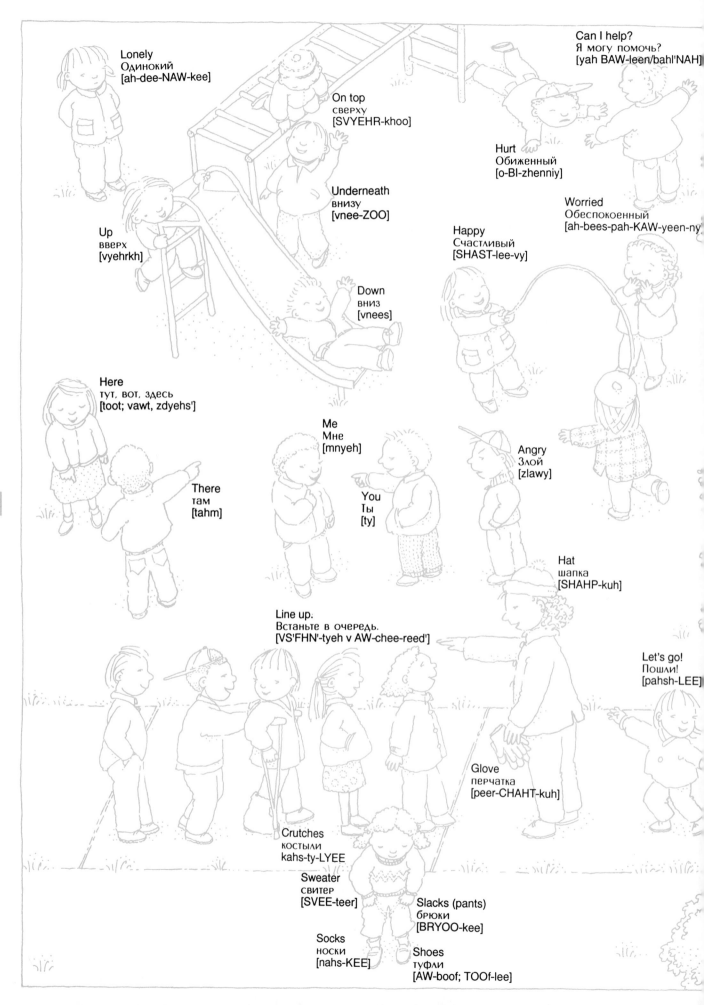

Lonely
Одинокий
[ah-dee-NAW-kee]

On top
сверху
[SVYEHR-khoo]

Underneath
внизу
[vnee-ZOO]

Up
вверх
[vyehrkh]

Down
вниз
[vnees]

Can I help?
Я могу помочь?
[yah BAW-leen/bahl'NAH]

Hurt
Обиженный
[o-BI-zhenniy]

Worried
Обеспокоенный
[ah-bees-pah-KAW-yeen-ny]

Happy
Счастливый
[SHAST-lee-vy]

Here
тут, вот, здесь
[toot; vawt, zdyehs']

There
там
[tahm]

Me
Мне
[mnyeh]

You
Ты
[ty]

Angry
Злой
[zlawy]

Hat
шапка
[SHAHP-kuh]

Line up.
Встаньте в очередь.
[VS'FHN'-tyeh v AW-chee-reed']

Let's go!
Пошли!
[pahsh-LEE]

Glove
перчатка
[peer-CHAHT-kuh]

Crutches
костыли
kahs-ty-LYEE

Sweater
свитер
[SVEE-teer]

Slacks (pants)
брюки
[BRYOO-kee]

Socks
носки
[nahs-KEE]

Shoes
туфли
[AW-boof; TOOf-lee]

42

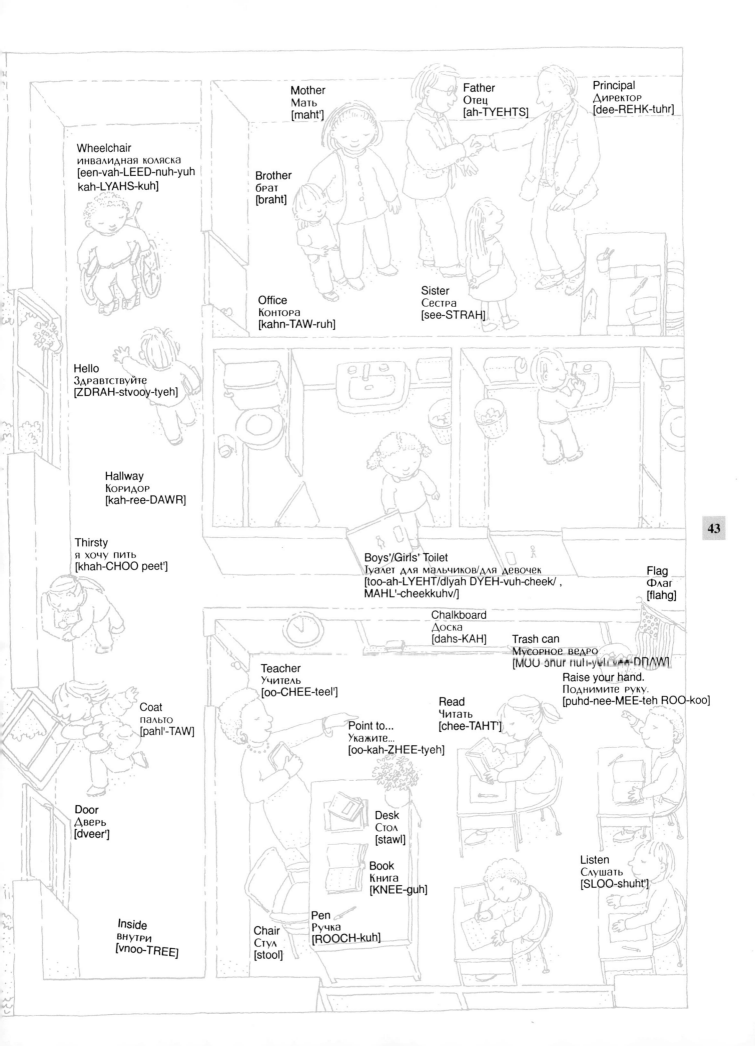

Wheelchair
инвалидная коляска
[een-vah-LEED-nuh-yuh
kah-LYAHS-kuh]

Hello
Здравствуйте
[ZDRAH-stvooy-tyeh]

Hallway
Коридор
[kah-ree-DAWR]

Thirsty
я хочу пить
[khah-CHOO peet']

Coat
пальто
[pahl'-TAW]

Door
Дверь
[dveer']

Inside
внутри
[vnoo-TREE]

Mother
Мать
[maht']

Brother
брат
[braht]

Office
Контора
[kahn-TAW-ruh]

Father
Отец
[ah-TYEHTS]

Sister
Сестра
[see-STRAH]

Principal
Директор
[dee-REHK-tuhr]

Boys'/Girls' Toilet
Туалет для мальчиков/для девочек
[too-ah-LYEHT/dlyah DYEH-vuh-cheek/,
MAHL'-cheekkuhv/]

Flag
Флаг
[flahg]

Chalkboard
Доска
[dahs-KAH]

Trash can
Мусорное ведро
[MOO-shur nuh-yeh vee-DRAW]

Raise your hand.
Поднимите руку.
[puhd-nee-MEE-teh ROO-koo]

Teacher
Учитель
[oo-CHEE-teel']

Point to...
Укажите...
[oo-kah-ZHEE-tyeh]

Read
Читать
[chee-TAHT']

Desk
Стол
[stawl]

Book
Книга
[KNEE-guh]

Listen
Слушать
[SLOO-shuht']

Pen
Ручка
[ROOCH-kuh]

Chair
Стул
[stool]

43

44

Excuse me.
Извините.
[ee-zvee-NEE-tyeh]

Eyeglasses
очки
[ahch-KEE]

That's better!
Это лучше!
[EH-tuh Loo-cheh]

Closet
Стенной шкаф
[stee-NOY shkahf]

Thank you
Спасибо
[spah-SEE-buh]

I needhelp.
Помогите мне.
[puh-mah-GEE-tyeh mnyeh]

Stand up.
Встаньте.
[VSTAN'-tyeh]

Pencil
Карандаш
[kah-rahn-DAHSH]

Good!
Хорошо!
[khah-rah-SHAW]

Tired
Уставший
[oos-TAHV-shy]

Table
Стол
[stawl]

Paper
Бумага
[boo-MAH-guh]

Shelf
Полка
[PAWL-kuh]

Can I borrow that?
Можно одолжить?
[MAWZH-nuh ah-dahl-ZHYT']

Yes
да
[dah]

Come here.
Идите сюда.
[ee-TEE syoo-DAH]

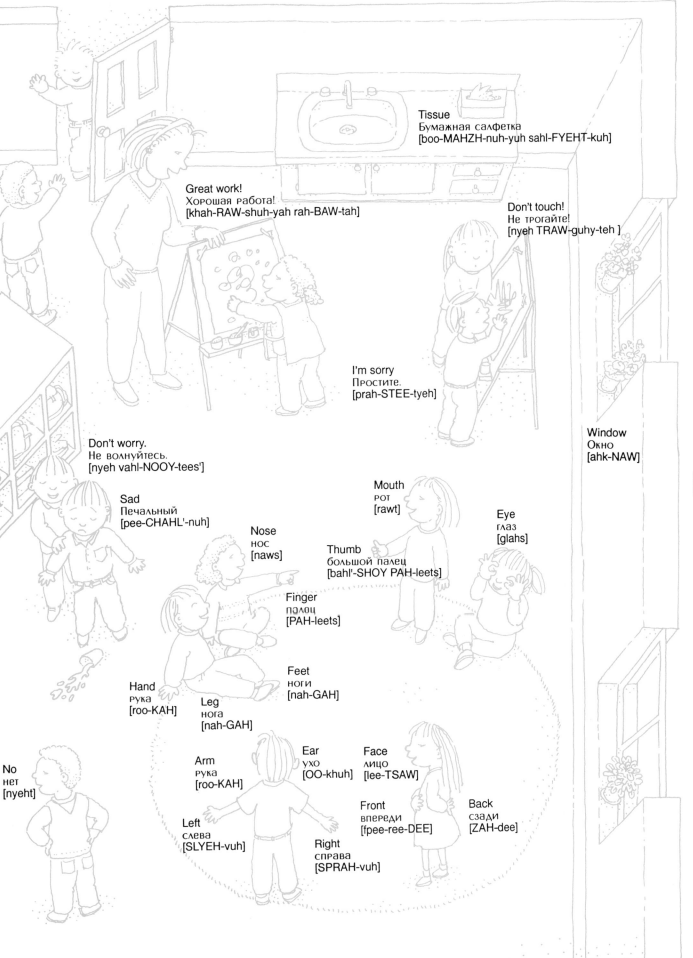

Lonely
Usamljen
[OO-sah-mehl-yehn]

On top
Na vrhu
[nah VEHR-HOO]

Hurt
Povrijedjen
[poh-VREE-jehn]

Can I help?
Da li mogu pomoći?
[DAH LEE maw-goo
paw-maw-CHEE]

Underneath
Ispod
[is-pod]

Worried
Zabrinut
[zah-BREE-noot]

Happy
Sretan
[SRAY-ton]

Up
Gore
[gaw-reh]

Down
Dolje
[DOHL-yeh]

Here
Ovdje
[ov-DEE-ay]

There
Tamo
[tah-moh]

Me
Mene
[MEN-eh]

You
Ti
[tee]

Angry
Ljut
[loot]

Hat
Kaoa
[kah-pah]

Line up.
Postroji se.
[poh-STROI-yee seh]

Let's go!
Idemo!
[EE-deh-moh]

Glove
Rukavica
[roo-kah-VEE-tzah]

Crutches
Stake
[SHTAH-keh]

Sweater
Vesta
[ves-tah]

Slacks (pants)
Hlace
[hil-ACH-eh]

Socks
Carape
[chah-RAHP-EH]

Shoes
Cipele
[TZEE-peh-leh]

46

Principal
Direktor skole
[dih-REHCK- tor SHKOL-eh]

Mother
Majka
[MY-kah]

Father
Otac
[OH-tahtz]

Wheelchair
Invalidska kolica
[in-vah-LEED-skah
koh-LEE-tzah]

Brother
Brat
[braht]

Office
Ured
[OO-rehd]

Sister
Sestra
[SEHS-trah]

Hallway
Hodnik
[hod-nihk]

47

Thirsty
Zedan
[JAY-dahn]

Boys'/Girls' toilet
Muski/Zenski zahod
[MOOSHI-kee/jen-skee, za-Zenski zahod
hohd]

Flag
Zastava
[ZAHS-ta vah]

Trash can
Kanta za smece
[KAHN-tah ZA
smeh-CHAY]

Chalkboard
Tabla
[TAH-blah]

Coat
Kaput
[CAH-poot]

Teacher
Ucitelj
[OOCH-eh-tehl]

Point to...
Pokazati...
[POH-kah-zah-tee]

Read
Citati
[CHEE-tah-tay]

Raise your hand.
Digni ruku!
[dihg-NEE roo-koo]

Desk
Klupa
[KLOO-pah]

Door
Vrata
[VRAH-tah]

Book
Knjiga
[K-NEE-gah]

Listen
Slusati
[SLOO-shah-tay]

Pen
Pero
[PEH-roh]

Inside
Iznutra
[iz-noo-TRAH]

Chair
Stolica
[STAW-lee-tzah]

Excuse me.
Izvinite.
[ihz-veen-ee-teh]

Eyeglasses
Naocale
[NAO-OH-chah-leh]

That's better.
To je bolje.
[toh-yeh BOHL-yah]

Closet
Spremnica
[SPREHM-nee-tza]

Thank you
Hvala
[HEHR-ah-lah]

I need help.
Potrebna mi je pomoc.
[POH-treb-nah mee YEH]

Stand up.
Sjedi.
[oo-STAH-nee]

Pencil
Olovka
[aw-lov-kah]

Good
Dobro
[daw-braw]

Tired
Umoran
[OO-maw-ran]

Table
Sto
[stoh]

Paper
Papir
[pah-PIHR]

Come here.
Dodji ovdje.
[dod-JEE awv-dah-yeh]

Shelf
Polica
[PAW-LEE-tzah]

Can I borrow that?
Da li mogu to posuditi?
[DAH LEE moh-goo toh poh-soo-dih-TEE]

Yes
Da
[dah]

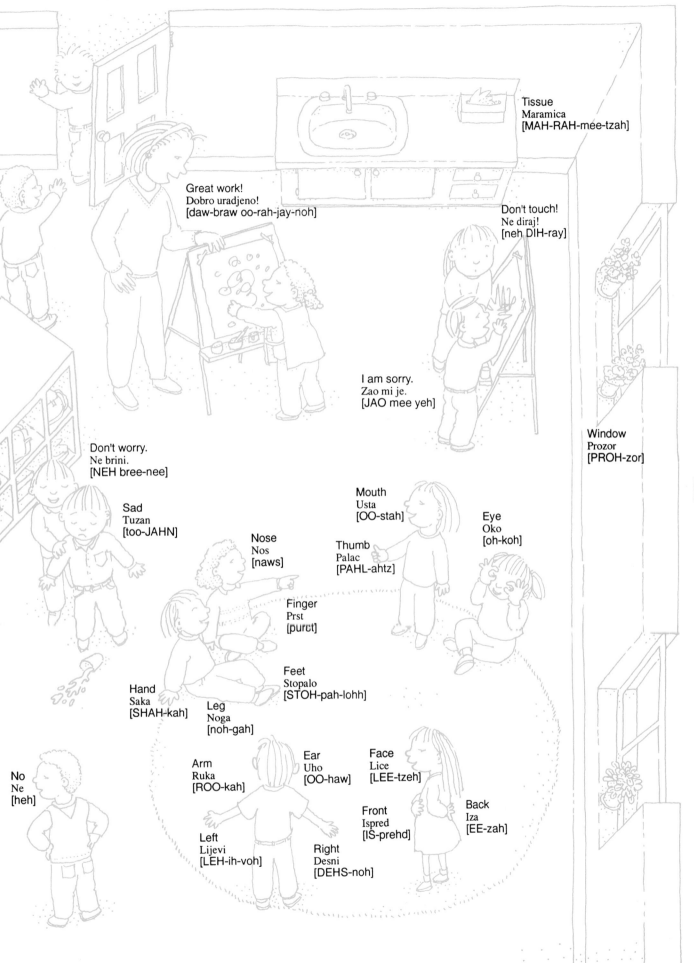

Tissue
Maramica
[MAH-RAH-mee-tzah]

Great work!
Dobro uradjeno!
[daw-braw oo-rah-jay-noh]

Don't touch!
Ne diraj!
[neh DIH-ray]

I am sorry.
Zao mi je.
[JAO mee yeh]

Window
Prozor
[PROH-zor]

Don't worry.
Ne brini.
[NEH bree-nee]

Sad
Tuzan
[too-JAHN]

Mouth
Usta
[OO-stah]

Eye
Oko
[oh-koh]

Nose
Nos
[naws]

Thumb
Palac
[PAHL-ahtz]

Finger
Prst
[purct]

Feet
Stopalo
[STOH-pah-lohh]

Hand
Saka
[SHAH-kah]

Leg
Noga
[noh-gah]

Arm
Ruka
[ROO-kah]

Ear
Uho
[OO-haw]

Face
Lice
[LEE-tzeh]

Front
Ispred
[IS-prehd]

Back
Iza
[EE-zah]

No
Ne
[heh]

Left
Lijevi
[LEH-ih-voh]

Right
Desni
[DEHS-noh]

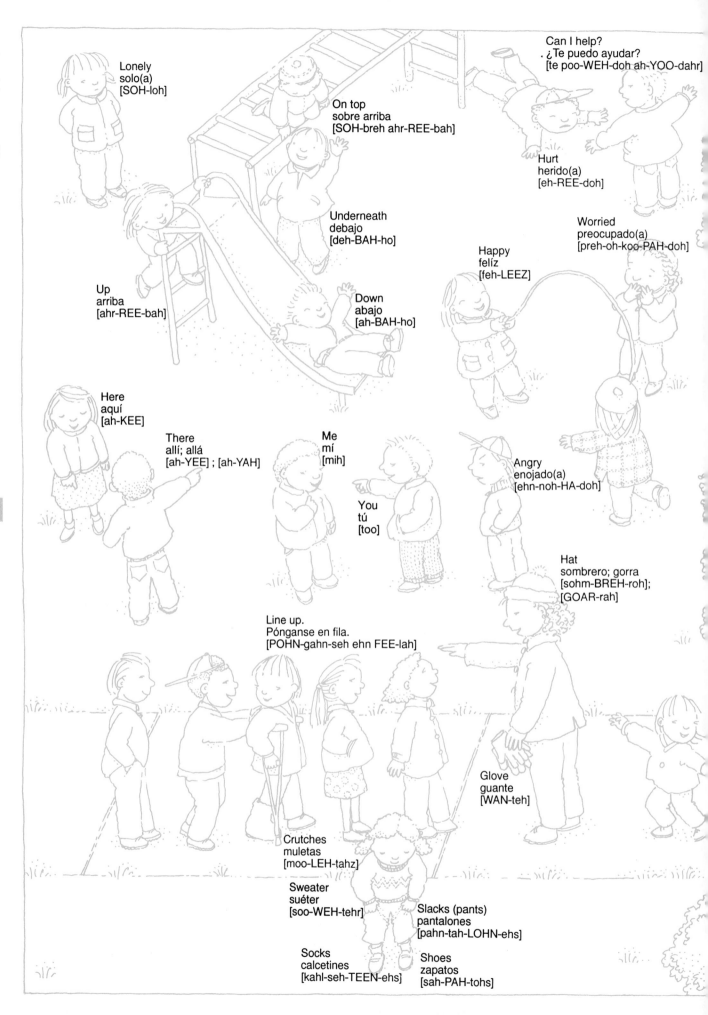

Lonely
solo(a)
[SOH-loh]

On top
sobre arriba
[SOH-breh ahr-REE-bah]

Underneath
debajo
[deh-BAH-ho]

Up
arriba
[ahr-REE-bah]

Down
abajo
[ah-BAH-ho]

Can I help?
¿Te puedo ayudar?
[te poo-WEH-doh ah-YOO-dahr]

Hurt
herido(a)
[eh-REE-doh]

Worried
preocupado(a)
[preh-oh-koo-PAH-doh]

Happy
felíz
[feh-LEEZ]

Here
aquí
[ah-KEE]

There
allí; allá
[ah-YEE] ; [ah-YAH]

Me
mí
[mih]

You
tú
[too]

Angry
enojado(a)
[ehn-noh-HA-doh]

Hat
sombrero; gorra
[sohm-BREH-roh];
[GOAR-rah]

Line up.
Pónganse en fila.
[POHN-gahn-seh ehn FEE-lah]

Glove
guante
[WAN-teh]

Crutches
muletas
[moo-LEH-tahz]

Sweater
suéter
[soo-WEH-tehr]

Slacks (pants)
pantalones
[pahn-tah-LOHN-ehs]

Socks
calcetines
[kahl-seh-TEEN-ehs]

Shoes
zapatos
[sah-PAH-tohs]

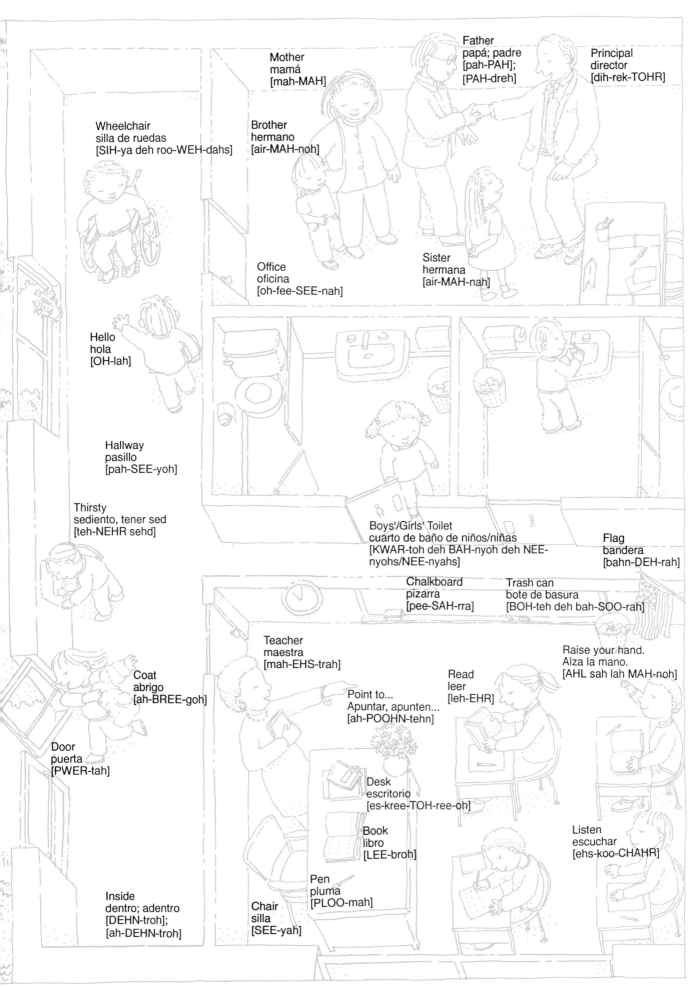

Wheelchair
silla de ruedas
[SIH-ya deh roo-WEH-dahs]

Mother
mamá
[mah-MAH]

Brother
hermano
[air-MAH-noh]

Father
papá; padre
[pah-PAH];
[PAH-dreh]

Principal
director
[dih-rek-TOHR]

Office
oficina
[oh-fee-SEE-nah]

Sister
hermana
[air-MAH-nah]

Hello
hola
[OH-lah]

Hallway
pasillo
[pah-SEE-yoh]

Thirsty
sediento, tener sed
[teh-NEHR sehd]

Boys'/Girls' Toilet
cuarto de baño de niños/niñas
[KWAR-toh deh BAH-nyoh deh NEE-
nyohs/NEE-nyahs]

Flag
bandera
[bahn-DEH-rah]

Chalkboard
pizarra
[pee-SAH-rra]

Trash can
bote de basura
[BOH-teh deh bah-SOO-rah]

Coat
abrigo
[ah-BREE-goh]

Teacher
maestra
[mah-EHS-trah]

Point to...
Apuntar, apunten...
[ah-POOHN-tehn]

Read
leer
[leh-EHR]

Raise your hand.
Alza la mano.
[AHL sah lah MAH-noh]

Door
puerta
[PWER-tah]

Desk
escritorio
[es-kree-TOH-ree-oh]

Book
libro
[LEE-broh]

Listen
escuchar
[ehs-koo-CHAHR]

Pen
pluma
[PLOO-mah]

Inside
dentro; adentro
[DEHN-troh];
[ah-DEHN-troh]

Chair
silla
[SEE-yah]

51

Excuse me.
Perdóname; Disculpeme; Con su permiso
[pehr-DOHN-ah-meh]
[dees-KOOHL-peh-meh]
[kohn soo pehr-MEE-soh]

Eyeglasses
gafas; anteojos
[GAH-fahz];
[ahn-teh-O-hos]

That's better!
¡Mucho mejor!
[MOO-cho meh-HOAR]

Closet
guardarropa
[wahr-dah-RROH-pah]

Thank you
Gracias
[GRAH-see-ahs]

I need help.
Necesito ayuda.
[neh-seh-SEE-toh ah-YOO-dah]

Stand up.
Pónganse de pie.
[POHN-gahn-seh deh pee-EH]

Pencil
lápiz
[LAH-peehz]

Good!
¡Muy bién!
[mooy bee-EHN]

Tired
cansado(a)
[kan-SAH-doh]

Table
mesa
[MEH-sah]

Paper
papel
[pah-PEHL]

Shelf
estante
[ehs-TAHN-teh]

Can I borrow that?
¿Me prestas esto?
[meh PREHZ-tahz EHS-toh]

Yes
sí
[SEE]

Come here.
Ven aquí
[vehn ah-KEE]

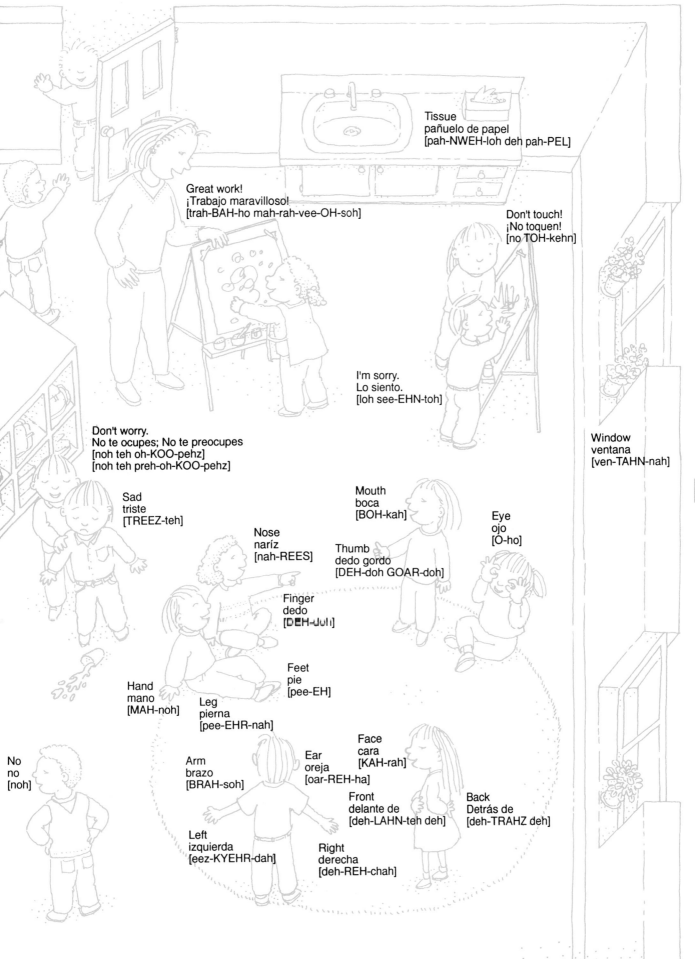

Tissue
pañuelo de papel
[pah-NWEH-loh deh pah-PEL]

Great work!
¡Trabajo maravilloso!
[trah-BAH-ho mah-rah-vee-OH-soh]

Don't touch!
¡No toquen!
[no TOH-kehn]

I'm sorry.
Lo siento.
[loh see-EHN-toh]

Don't worry.
No te ocupes; No te preocupes
[noh teh oh-KOO-pehz]
[noh teh preh-oh-KOO-pehz]

Window
ventana
[ven-TAHN-nah]

53

Sad
triste
[TREEZ-teh]

Mouth
boca
[BOH-kah]

Eye
ojo
[O-ho]

Nose
naríz
[nah-REES]

Thumb
dedo gordo
[DEH-doh GOAR-doh]

Finger
dedo
[DEH-Joh]

Feet
pie
[pee-EH]

Hand
mano
[MAH-noh]

Leg
pierna
[pee-EHR-nah]

Face
cara
[KAH-rah]

Arm
brazo
[BRAH-soh]

Ear
oreja
[oar-REH-ha]

No
no
[noh]

Front
delante de
[deh-LAHN-teh deh]

Back
Detrás de
[deh-TRAHZ deh]

Left
izquierda
[eez-KYEHR-dah]

Right
derecha
[deh-REH-chah]

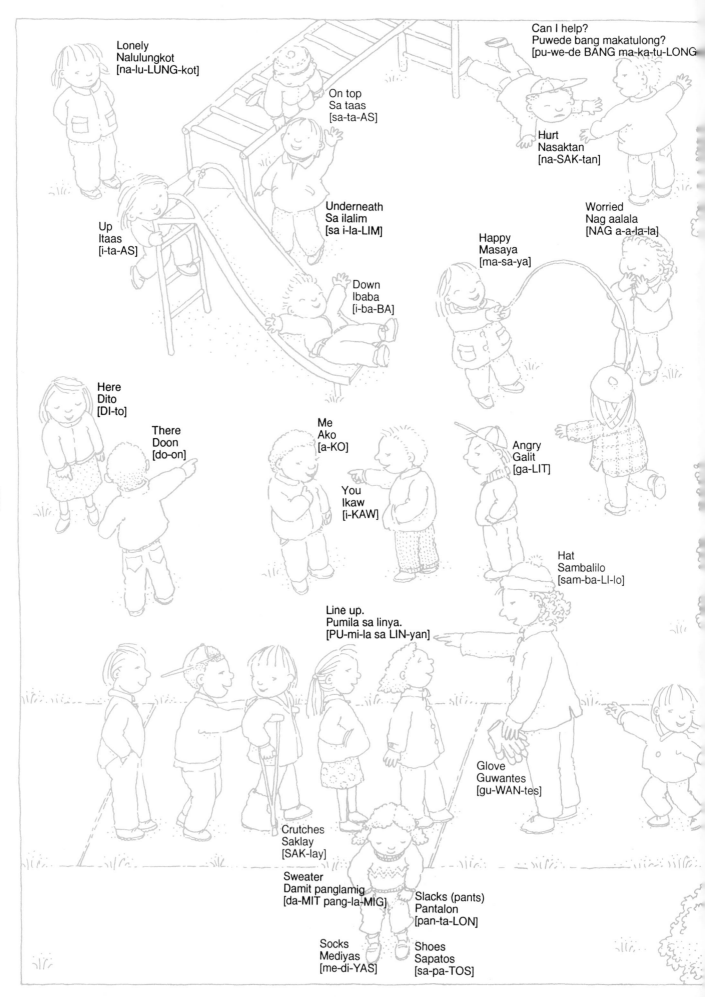

Lonely
Nalulungkot
[na-lu-LUNG-kot]

On top
Sa taas
[sa-ta-AS]

Can I help?
Puwede bang makatulong?
[pu-we-de BANG ma-ka-tu-LONG

Hurt
Nasaktan
[na-SAK-tan]

Underneath
Sa ilalim
[sa i-la-LIM]

Worried
Nag aalala
[NAG a-a-la-la]

Up
Itaas
[i-ta-AS]

Happy
Masaya
[ma-sa-ya]

Down
Ibaba
[i-ba-BA]

Here
Dito
[DI-to]

There
Doon
[do-on]

Me
Ako
[a-KO]

Angry
Galit
[ga-LIT]

You
Ikaw
[i-KAW]

Hat
Sambalilo
[sam-ba-LI-lo]

Line up.
Pumila sa linya.
[PU-mi-la sa LIN-yan]

Glove
Guwantes
[gu-WAN-tes]

Crutches
Saklay
[SAK-lay]

Sweater
Damit panglamig
[da-MIT pang-la-MIG]

Slacks (pants)
Pantalon
[pan-ta-LON]

Socks
Mediyas
[me-di-YAS]

Shoes
Sapatos
[sa-pa-TOS]

54

Wheelchair
Upuan na maygulong
[u-PU-an na may-gu-LONG]

Mother
Ina
[i-NA]

Brother
Kapatid na lalaki
[ka-pa-TID na la-la-KI]

Father
Ama
[a-MA]

Principal
Punong buro
[pu-NONG GU-ro]

Office
Opisina
[o-pi-SI-na]

Sister
Kapatid na babae
[ka-pa-TID na ba-ba-E]

Hello
Kumusta
[ku-MUS-ta]

Hallway
Daanan ng tad
[da-a-nan NG ta-O]

55

Thirsty
Uhaw
[u-HAW]

Boys'/Girls' Toilet
Lalaki/babae palikuran
[la-la-KI/ba-ba-E pa-li-KU-ran]

Flag
Bandila
[ban-DI-la]

Chalkboard
Pisara
[PI-sa-ra]

Trash can
Basurahan
[ba-SU-ra-han]

Coat
Damit panglamig
[da-MIT pang-la-MIG]

Teacher
Guro
[GU-ro]

Point to...
Ituro...
[i-TU-ro]

Read
Magbasa
[MAG-ba-sa]

Raise your hand.
Itaas ang kamay.
[I-ta-as ANG ka-may]

Door
Pintuan
[pin-TU-an]

Desk
Mesang sulutan
[me-SANG su-la-tan]

Book
Libro
[LIB-ro]

Listen
Making
[ma-KI-nig]

Pen
Pluma
[PLU-ma]

Inside
Sa loob
[sa lo-ob]

Chair
Upan
[u-PU-an]

Eyeglasses
Salamin sa mata
[sa-la-MIN sa ma-TA]

That's better!
Magaling mo uli!
[ga-wa-IN mo u-LI]

Closet
Aparador
[a-pa-ra-DO

Excuse me.
Makikiraan.
[ma-KI-KI-ra-an]

Thank you
Salamat
[sa-la-MAT]

Stand up.
Tumayo
[TU-na-yo]

I need help.
Kailangan ko ang tulong.
[ka-I-la-ngan ko ang tu-LONG

Pencil
Lapis
[la-PIS]

Good!
Magaling!
[maga-LING]

Tired
Pagod
[pa-GOD]

Table
Mesa
[me-sa]

Paper
Papel
[pa-pel]

Shelf
Lalagyan ng libro
[la-lag-yan ng LI-bro]

Can I borrow that?
Puwede bang mahiram iyan?
[pu-we-de BANG ma-hi-RAM I-yan]

Come here.
Halika rito.
[ha-LI-ka RI-to]

Yes
O, o
[oh-oh]

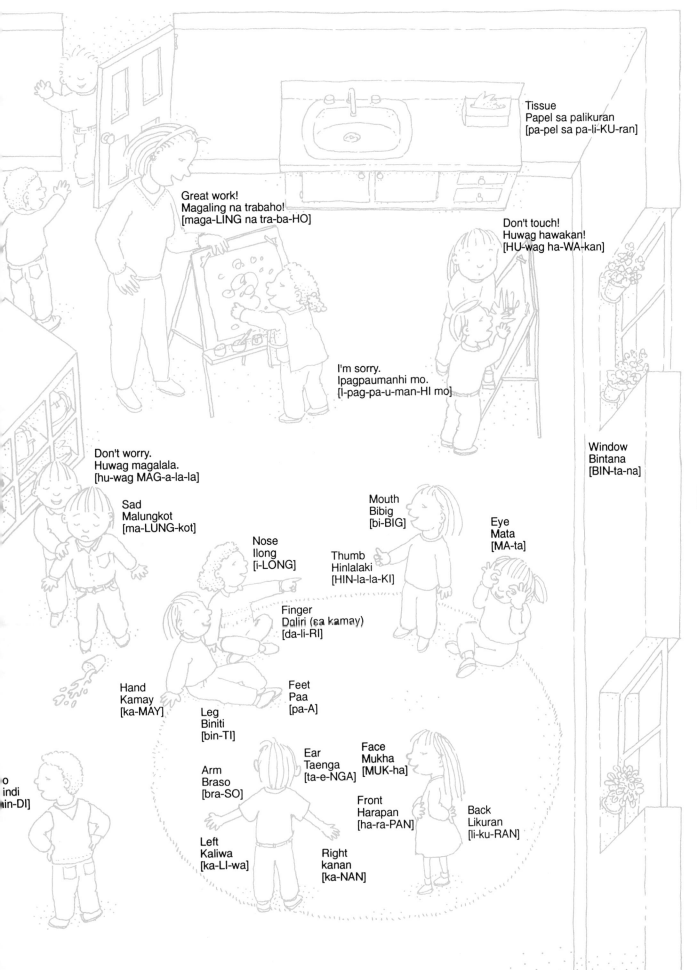

Tissue
Papel sa palikuran
[pa-pel sa pa-li-KU-ran]

Great work!
Magaling na trabaho!
[maga-LING na tra-ba-HO]

Don't touch!
Huwag hawakan!
[HU-wag ha-WA-kan]

I'm sorry.
Ipagpaumanhi mo.
[I-pag-pa-u-man-HI mo]

Window
Bintana
[BIN-ta-na]

Don't worry.
Huwag magalala.
[hu-wag MAG-a-la-la]

Sad
Malungkot
[ma-LUNG-kot]

Mouth
Bibig
[bi-BIG]

Eye
Mata
[MA-ta]

Nose
Ilong
[i-LONG]

Thumb
Hinlalaki
[HIN-la-la-KI]

Finger
Daliri (sa kamay)
[da-li-RI]

Hand
Kamay
[ka-MAY]

Feet
Paa
[pa-A]

Leg
Biniti
[bin-TI]

Ear
Taenga
[ta-e-NGA]

Face
Mukha
[MUK-ha]

Arm
Braso
[bra-SO]

Front
Harapan
[ha-ra-PAN]

Back
Likuran
[li-ku-RAN]

o
indi
in-DI]

Left
Kaliwa
[ka-LI-wa]

Right
kanan
[ka-NAN]

Lonely
تنہا
[tun-HAH]

on top
سب سے اوپر
[KAY OO-purr]

Hurt
دکھا ہوا
[doo-KAH hoo-AH]

Can I help?
کیا میں مدد کر سکتا ہوں
[kyah MAYN mah-DAHD cur SAHK-tah HOON]

underneath
نیچے
[nee-CHAY]

up
اوپر
[OO-purr]

Worried
پریشان
[pree-SHAN]

Happy
خوش
[khoish]

down
نیچے
[nee-CHAY]

here
یہاں
[yah-HAHN]

me
مجھے
[moo-JAY]

there
وہاں
[wah-HAHN]

you
تم
[toom]

Angry
غصہ میں
[ghoo-say MEHN]

hat
ٹوپی
[toh-PEE]

Line up.
لائن بناؤ
[LYNE bah-NAO]

Let's go?
چلو چلیں
[chah-LOH CHAH-lehn]

glove
دستانہ
[dus-TAH-NAY]

crutches
بیساکھی کے چلنے کی بیساکھیاں
[beh-sah-KEE]

sweater
سویٹر
[Same as English]

slacks (pants)
پتلون
[pat-LOON]

socks
موزہ
[moh-zay]

shoes
جوتے
[joo-tay]

58

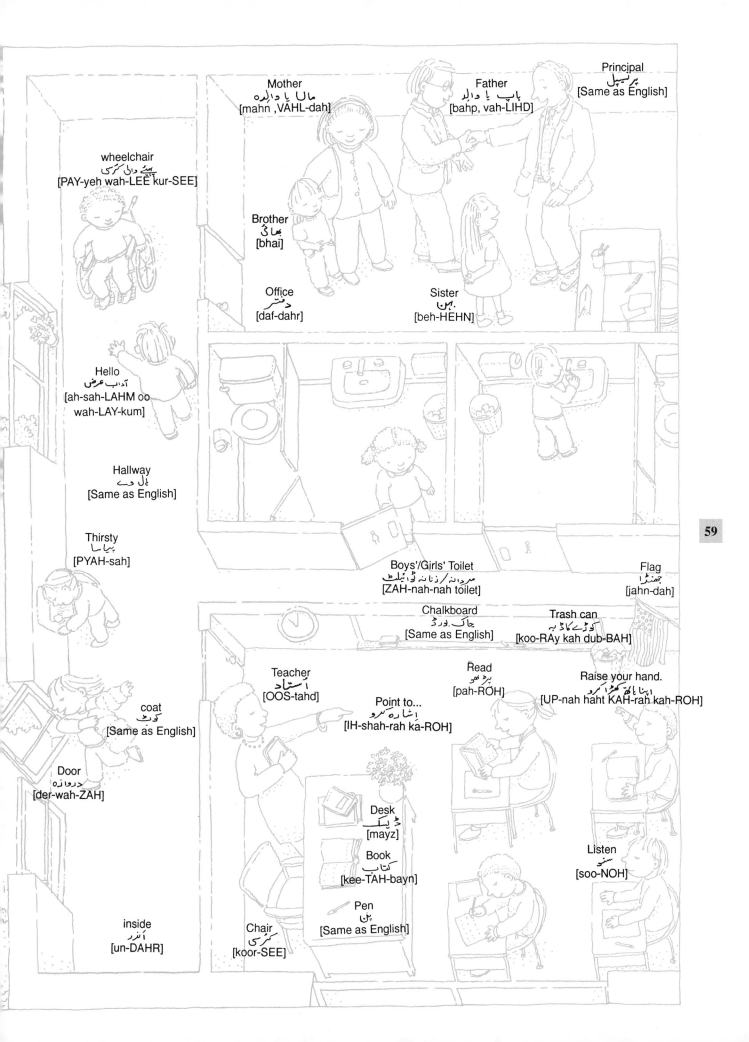

Principal
پرنسپل
[Same as English]

Mother
ماں یا والدہ
[mahn, VAHL-dah]

Father
باپ یا والد
[bahp, vah-LIHD]

wheelchair
پہیے والی کرسی
[PAY-yeh wah-LEE kur-SEE]

Brother
بھائی
[bhai]

Office
دفتر
[daf-dahr]

Sister
بہن
[beh-HEHN]

Hello
آداب عرض
[ah-sah-LAHM oo wah-LAY-kum]

Hallway
ہال وے
[Same as English]

Thirsty
پیاسا
[PYAH-sah]

Boys'/Girls' Toilet
مردانہ/زنانہ ٹوائلٹ
[ZAH-nah-nah toilet]

Flag
جھنڈا
[jahn-dah]

Chalkboard
چاک بورڈ
[Same as English]

Trash can
کوڑے کا ڈبہ
[koo-RAy kah dub-BAH]

coat
کوٹ
[Same as English]

Teacher
اُستاد
[OOS-tahd]

Point to...
اِشارہ کرو
[IH-shah-rah ka-ROH]

Read
پڑھو
[pah-ROH]

Raise your hand.
اپنا ہاتھ کھڑا کرو
[UP-nah haht KAH-rah kah-ROH]

Door
دروازہ
[der-wah-ZAH]

Desk
ڈیسک
[mayz]

Book
کتاب
[kee-TAH-bayn]

Listen
سنو
[soo-NOH]

Pen
پین
[Same as English]

inside
اندر
[un-DAHR]

Chair
کرسی
[koor-SEE]

59

eyeglasses
چشمہ
[CHAWSH-mah]

That's better!
یہ بہتر ہے
[yeh beh-TAHR HAY]

Closet
الماری
[ahl-mah-RE

Excuse me.
معاف کیجیۓ
[mahf kee-jee-AY]

Thank you
شکریہ
[shook-REE-ah]

I need help.
مجھے مدد چاہیۓ
[moo-JAY mah-DAHD chah-ee-ay]

Stand up.
کھڑے ہو جاؤ
[kah-RAY hoh-JAO]

Pencil
پنسل
[Same as English]

Good!
شاباش ۔ بہت اچھا
[shah-bahsh]

Tired
تھکا ہوا
[tah-KAH HOO-ah]

Table
کرسی
[mayz]

Paper
کاغذ
[kah-Guz]

Shelf
شیلف
[TAHK-tay]

Can I borrow that?
کیا میں یہ لے سکتا ہوں
[kyah MAYN woh oo-DAHR LAY sahk-tah HOON]

yes
جی
[jee]

Come here.
یہاں آؤ
[yah-HAHN ah-oh]

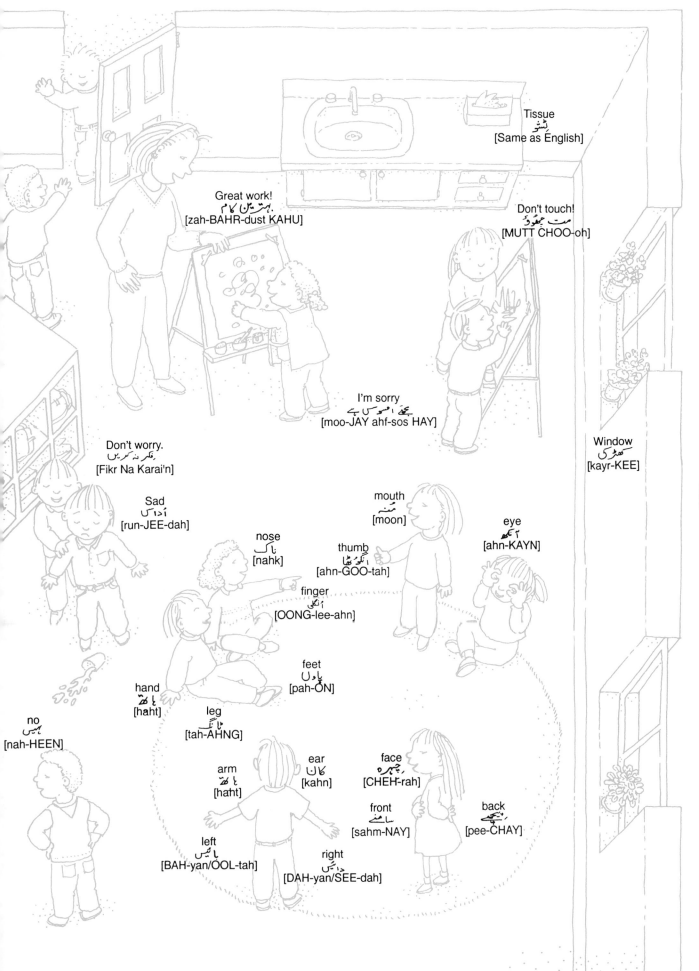

Tissue
رسشو
[Same as English]

Great work!
بہترین کام
[zah-BAHR-dust KAHU]

Don't touch!
مت چھوؤ
[MUTT CHOO-oh]

I'm sorry
مجھے افسوس ہے
[moo-JAY ahf-sos HAY]

Window
کھڑکی
[kayr-KEE]

Don't worry.
فکر نہ کریں
[Fikr Na Karai'n]

Sad
اُداس
[run-JEE-dah]

mouth
مُنہ
[moon]

eye
آنکھ
[ahn-KAYN]

nose
ناک
[nahk]

thumb
انگوٹھا
[ahn-GOO-tah]

finger
اُنگلی
[OONG-lee-ahn]

feet
پاؤں
[pah-ON]

hand
ہاتھ
[haht]

leg
ٹانگ
[tah-AHNG]

no
نہیں
[nah-HEEN]

arm
بازو
[haht]

ear
کان
[kahn]

face
چہرہ
[CHEH-rah]

front
سامنے
[sahm-NAY]

back
پیچھے
[pee-CHAY]

left
بائیں
[BAH-yan/OOL-tah]

right
دائیں
[DAH-yan/SEE-dah]

Lonely
Cô đơn
[goh dawn]

On top
Ở trên
[aw chehn]

Can I help?
Cần gì không?
[gahn zee kawng]

Underneath
Ở dướiaw
[zoh-ee]

Hurt
Đau khổ
[dao koh]

Up
Lên
[lehn]

Worried
Lo âu
[law au]

Happy
Vui
[voo-i]

Down
Xuống
[shoo-awn]

Here
Ở đây
[aw dye]

There
Kia
[geh-ih]

You (male/female)
Anh/Chị
[ahn/jay]

Me
Tôi
[doi]

Angry
Giận
[yahn]

Hat
Nón
[non]

Line up.
Sắp hàng.
[sahp hang]

Let's go.
Đi thôi.
[day toi]

Glove
Bao tay
[bao dye]

Crutches
Nạng
[nahng]

Sweater
Áo lạnh
[ao lahn]

Slacks (pants)
Quần
[gwahn]

Socks
Vớ
[vaw]

Shoes
Giày
[zah-ee]

Wheelchair
Xe lăn
[shay lahn]

Mother
Mẹ
[meh]

Brother
Anh/Em
[ahn/ehm]

Father
Cha
[jah]

Principal
Hiệu trưởng
[hyoo choong]

Office
Văn phòng
[vahn fawng]

Sister
Chị/Em
[jay/ehm]

Hello
Mạnh giỏi
[mahn yoi]

Hallway
Hành lang
[hahn lahng]

Thirsty
Khát
[kaht]

Boys' / Girls' toilet
Phòng tắm nam /nữ
[fawng dahm nahm / noo]

Flag
Cờ
[goh]

Chalkboard
Bảng đen
[bahn dehn]

Trash can
Thùng rác
[toong rak]

Teacher
Thầy giáo
[tye zao]

Point to...
Chỉ vào...
[jay vaw]

Read
Đọc
[dawk]

Raise your hand.
Đưa tay lên.
[doo dye lehn]

Coat
Áo khoác
[ao kwock]

Desk
Bàn học
[bahn hawk]

Door
Cửa
[gih]

Book
Sách
[sahk]

Listen
Nghe
[hneh]

Inside
Trong
[chawng]

Chair
Ghế
[gay]

Pen
Viết
[Vee-eht]

63

Excuse me
Xin lỗi
[sihn loi]

Eyeglasses
Mắt kiếng
[maht kee-ehm]

That's better.
Khá hơn.
[kah hoon]

Closet
Tủ
[doh]

Stand up.
Đứng dậy.
[doong zye]

Thank you
Cám ơn
[gahm awn]

I need help.
Xin giúp tôi.
[sihn joop doi]

Pencil
Viết chì
[vee-eht jay]

Good
Tốt lắm
[dawt lahm]

Tired
Mệt
[meht]

Table
Bàn
[bahn]

Paper
Giấy
[zye]

Can I borrow?
Tôi có thể mượn không?
[doi goh tay moon kahng]

Shelf
Kệ
[geh]

Yes
Vâng
[vehng]

Come here.
Tới đây.
[doi dye]

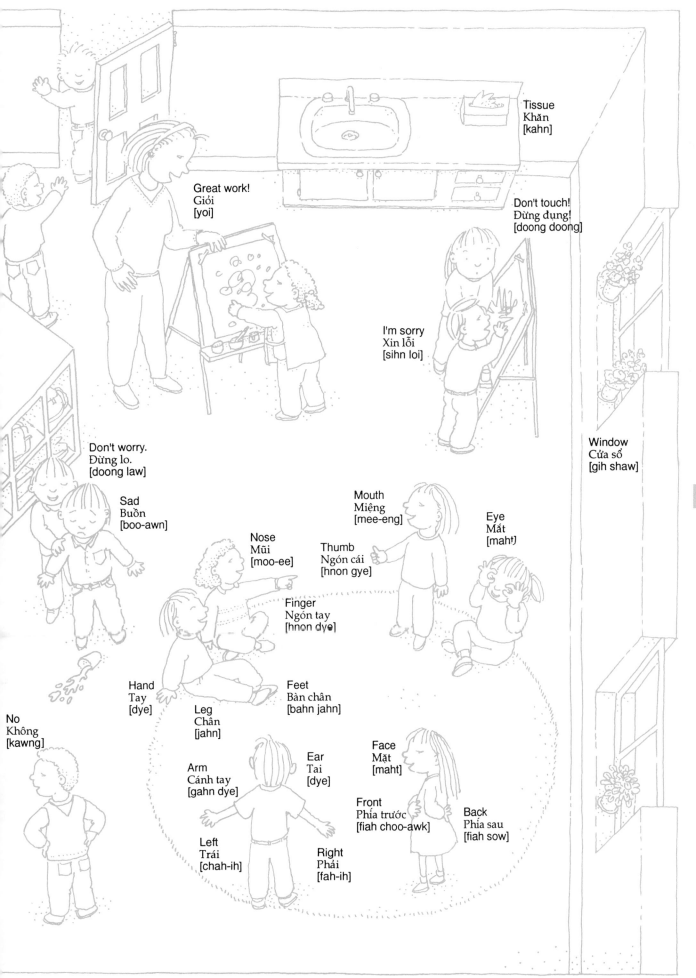

Tissue
Khăn
[kahn]

Great work!
Giỏi
[yoi]

Don't touch!
Đừng đụng!
[doong doong]

I'm sorry
Xin lỗi
[sihn loi]

Window
Cửa sổ
[gih shaw]

Don't worry.
Đừng lo.
[doong law]

Sad
Buồn
[boo-awn]

Mouth
Miệng
[mee-eng]

Eye
Mắt
[maht]

Nose
Mũi
[moo-ee]

Thumb
Ngón cái
[hnon gye]

Finger
Ngón tay
[hnon dye]

Hand
Tay
[dye]

Leg
Chân
[jahn]

Feet
Bàn chân
[bahn jahn]

No
Không
[kawng]

Arm
Cánh tay
[gahn dye]

Ear
Tai
[dye]

Face
Mặt
[maht]

Front
Phía trước
[fiah choo-awk]

Back
Phía sau
[fiah sow]

Left
Trái
[chah-ih]

Right
Phải
[fah-ih]

Arabic

English	Translation	Pronunciation
People		
I	انا	[a-nah]
You	أنتَ	[AHN-ta]
You (plural)	أنتم	[AHN-toom]
She	هي	[HAY-ya]
He	هو	[HOH-wah]
We	نحن	[NAH-noo]
They	هما	[hoh-MAH]
Them	هم	[hohm]
My name is...	إسمي	[EHS-mee]
Teacher	معلم	[moh-AHL-lehm]
Student	طالب	[tah-lehb]
Principal	مدير	[MOO-duhr]
Parent	والد	[wah-LEHD]
Mother	أم	[uhm]
Father	أب	[ahb]
Sister	أخت	[awkt]
Brother	أخ	[ahkh]
Parts of the Body		
Face	وجه	[wahgh]
Eye	عين	[ah-ihn]
Nose	أنف	[anf]
Mouth	فم	[fam]
Ear	أذن	[OH-don]
Hand	يد	[yad]
Finger	إصبع	[ihs-BAH]
Thumb	إبهام اليد	[ehb-HAM ehl-yahd]
Arm	ذراع	[zeh-RAH]
Leg	رجل	[rihg]
Feet	قدم	[KAW-dahm]
Clothing, "body furniture"		
Hat	قبعة	[koh-BAH]
Glove	قفاز	[koh-FAZ]
Eyeglasses	نظارات	[nah-ZAH-raht]
Wheelchair	كرسي متحرك	KUR-see MOO-daw-lahb]
Braces (teeth and leg)	مشبك أسنان حزام الرجل	[MASH-bak as-NAH] [heh-ZAHM ahl-RIHG]
Crutches	عكازات	[ah-KAH-zat]
Coat	معطف	[meh-tahf]
Sweater	كنزة	[KAHN-zah]
Shirt	قميص	[kah-MEES]
Slacks (pants)	بنطلون	[bahn-TAH-lawn]
Shoes	حذاء	[heh-ZAH]
Socks	جوارب	[gah-WAH-rehb]
Time		
Soon	حالا (قريبا)	[HA-lahn (kah-REE-bahn)]
Now	الآن	[ahl-AN]
Later	فيما بعد	[FEE-mah-bahd]
Today	اليوم	[ahl-YAWM]
This morning	هذا الصباح	[hah-ZAH SAH-baw]
This afternoon	(اليوم) بعد الظهر	[(ahl-YAH-hawn) bahd-ahl-ZOR]
Tonight	هذه الليلة	[ha-ZEE-heh ahl-LAY-lah]

Arabic

English	Arabic	Pronunciation
Excuse me.	غفراً	[ahf-wahn]
Manners		
Please	من فضلك	[mihn fahd-LAHK]
Thank you	شكراً	[SHOOK-rahn]
Yes	نعم	[nah-ahm]
No	لا (كلا)	[la/kah-LAH]
May I?	ممكن؟	[MOM-kehn]
I'm sorry.	أنا اسف	[ah-NAH ah-SEHF]
Feelings		
Hungry	جائع	[GAY-ah]
Angry	غاضب	[GHAH-dehb]
Lonely	وحيد	[wah-HEED]
Tired	تعبان	[tah-BAN]
Thirsty	عطشان	[AHCH-ahm]
Sad	حزين	[ha-ZEEN]
Happy	سعيد	[sah-EED]
Worried	موهوم	[mah-MOOM]
Hurt	مجروح	[maw-GOO-ah]
Commands/Requests		
Be quiet.	اسكت (سكتن)	[OS-kot (soo-KOOT)]
Don't run.	لا تركض	[LAH-tahr-kawd]
Stop!	قف!	[kehf]
Line up.	قف في صف	[KEHF fee sahf]
Stand up.	قف!	[Kehf]
Come here.	تعال هنا	[tah-AH-lah hoh-NAH]
Point to...	دل (على)	[dihl (AH-lah)]
Don't touch!	لا تلمس	[LAH TAHL-mehss]

English	Arabic	Pronunciation
Yesterday	أمس	[ams]
Tomorrow	غداً	[GHAH-dan]
Place		
Front	مقدمة / أمام	[moo-kah-DAY-mah/ah-MAM]
Back	خلف / مؤخرة	[moo-ahck-IH-rah/kahlf]
Up	في الأعلى	[fihl AH-lah]
Down	في الأسفل	[fihl AHS-fal]
On top	فوق	[fohk]
Underneath	تحت	[taht]
Here	هنا	hoh-NAH]
There	هناك	[hoh-NAK]
Inside	في الداخل	[fih DA-kehl]
In	في (داخل)	[fee]
Out	خارج	[KAH-rehg]
Left	يسار	[yah-SAHR]
Right	يمين	[yah-MEEN]
Human Relations		
Greetings,Goodbyes		
Hello	مرحبا	[mahr-HAH-bah]
Goodbye	مع السلامة	[mah-ah-SAH-leh-mah]
Can I help?	أي خدمة (مساعدة)؟	[I-kehd-mah/I-moo-sah-ah-DAH]
I feel sick.	أنا مريض	[ah-nah mah-REED]
Help me.	ساعدني	[sah-EHD-nee]
I love you.	أحبك	[oh-HEH-bok]
Do you need to use the bathroom?	هل تريد أن تذهب إلى الحمام؟	[hal toh-REED ahn tahz-hahb EHL-ahl el-hahm-MAM]
Don't worry.	لا تقلق	[lah tah-TAM]
Can I borrow that?	ممكن أستعير ذلك؟	[MOM-kehn ahs-TAH-ehr zah-LEHK]

I need help.	بحاجة إلى مساعدة	[beh-HAH-gah ehl-ah MOO-sah-ah-deh]
May I?	ممكن	[MOM-kehn]
Let's go!	لنذهب!	[lih-NAHZ-hahb]
Raise your hand	ارفع يدك	[ehr-FAH yah-DAHK]
Look	انظر!	[on-zor]

Affirmations/Negations

Good!	جيد	[GAH-yehd]
Great work!	عمل عظيم	[ah-MAFL ah-ZEEM]
That's better!	هذا افضل	[HAH-zah ahf-DAHL]
O.K.	ماشي	[MA-shee]

School and Classroom Furnishings

Desk	مقعد	[MAHK-ahd]
Chair	كرسي	[koor-SEE]
Table	طاولة	[TAHW-lah]
Chalkboard	لوح الطباشير	[lahw]
Flag	علم	[AH-lahm]
Door	باب	[bab]
Window	شباك	[sheh-BAK]
Closet	خزانة	[khah-ZA-nah]
Trash can	سلة المهملات	[sahl-LEHT AHL-moh mah-LAT]
Hallway	مدخل (قاعة)	[MAHD-kehl]
Office	مكتب	[MAHK-tahb]
Boys'/Girls' Toilet	حمام الطلاب/حمام الطالبات	[hah-MAM ehl-/TOHL-lahb/tah-LEE-beht]
Gym	نادي رياضي	[NA-dih REE-yah-dee]
Lunchroom	غرفة الغداء	[ghur-FEHT AHL-ghah-da]
Pen	قلم حبر	[kah-LAHM hehbr]

Pencil	قلم رصاص	[kah-LAHM rah-SAHS]
Paper	ورقة	[wah-RAHK]
Tissue	منديل	[mahn-DEEL]
Book	كتاب	[kih-TAHB]
Shelf	رف	[rahff]

School Activities

Homework	وظيفة	[wah-ZEE-fah]
Test	امتحان	[ihm-teh-HAN]
Report	تقرير	[tahk-RIHR]
Study	دراسة	[deh-REH-sah]
Read	اقرأ!	[ECK-rah]
Write	اكتب!	[OCK-tob]
Draw	ارسم!	[EHR-sehm]
Listen	استمع!	[ehss-TAH-meh]
Take this home to your parents.	خذ هذا إلى والديك في البيت	[kohz hah-ZAH EHL-ah wah-LEE-DYKE fihl-BYTE]

Bengali

English	Translation	Pronunciation
People		
I	অামি	[ah-MEE]
Me	অামি	[ah-MEE]
You	তুমি	[too-MEE]
You (plural)	তোমরা	[TOHM-rah]
She	সে	[shay]
He	সে	[Shay]
It	সে	[Shay]
We	অামরা	[AHM-rah]
Us	অামরা	[AHM-rah]
They	তারা	[TAH-rah]
Them	ওরা	[OH-rah]
My name is...	অামার নাম	[ah-MAHR nahm]
Teacher	শিক্ষক / শিক্ষিকা	[SHEE-kock/SHEE-KEE-kah]
Student	ছাত্র / ছাত্রী	[chah-TROH/Chah-TREE]
Principal	প্রধান	[prod-hahn]
Parent	অভিভাবক	[oh-bee-PAH-bok]
Mother	মা	[mah/ AHM-mah]
Father	বাবা	[bah-bah/ AHB-bah]
Sister	বোন	[bohn/AH-pah/ dee-dee]
Brother	ভাই	[bhai/dah-dah]
Parts of the Body		
Face	মুখ	[mookh]
Eye	চোখ	[chohkh]
Nose	নাক	[nahk]
Mouth	মুখ	[mookh]
Ear	কান	[kahn]
Hand	হাত	[haht]
Finger	আঙুল	[AHN-gool]
Thumb	বুড়ো আঙুল	[boo-roh AHN-gool]
Arm	বাহু	[BAH-hoo/haht]
Leg	পা	[pah]
Feet	পা	[pah]
Clothing, "body furniture"		
Hat	টুপি	[too-PEE]
Glove	দস্তানা	[DAWS-tah-nah]
Eyeglasses	চশমা	[CHAWSH-mah]
Wheelchair		Same as English
Braces (teeth and leg)	ব্রেসেস	Same as English
Crutches		Same as English
Coat	কোট	Same as English
Sweater	সোয়েটার	Same as English
Shirt	শার্ট	Same as English
Slacks (pants)	স্ল্যাকস	Same as English
Shoes	জুতো	[JOO-toh]
Socks	মোজা	[MOH-jah]
Time		
Soon	জলদি	[JOHL-dee]
Now	এখন	[ack-HOHN]
Later	পরে	[paw-ray]
Today	আজ	[ahj]
This morning	আজ সকালে	[ahj SHAW-kah-lay]
This afternoon	আজ দুপুরে	[ahj-DOO-paw-ray]
Tonight	আজ রাতে	[ahj-RAH-tay]

Yesterday	গতকাল	[go-TOH-kahl]
Tomorrow	আগামীকাল	[ah-GAH-MEE-kahl]
Place		
Front	সামনে	[SHAWM-nay]
Back	পিছনে	[pihch-WOH-nay]
Up	উপরে	[op-poh-F-AY]
Down	নীচে	[NEE-chay]
On top	সবার উপরে	[shaw-BAHR op-poh-RAY]
Underneath	সবার নীচে	[shaw-BAHR NEE-chay]
Here	এখানে	[eh-KAH-nay]
There	ওখানে	[oh-KAH-nay]
Inside	ভিতরে	[beh-toh-ray]
In	ভিতর	[bih-TOR]
Out	বাহির	[bah-HIHR]
Left	বাঁ	[bahn]
Right	ডান	[dahn]

Human Relations
Greetings, Goodbyes

Hello	নমস্কার/সালাম	[naw-mosh-KAHR/sah-LAHM]
Goodbye	খুদা হাফিজ্	[dah-kah HAW-bay]
Can I help?	আমি আপনাকে করতে পারি ?	[ah-MEE shah-hah-JOH kor-TAY pah-REE]
I feel sick.	আমার শরীর খারাপ লাগছে।	[ah-MAHR SHOH-rir kah-RAHP LAHG-chay]
Help me.	আমাকে সাহায্য করো।	[ah-my shah-hah-JOH kaw-RO]
I love you.	আমি তোমাকে ভালোবাসি	[ah-MEE to-MAH-kay bah-LOH-bak-SHEE]
Do you need to use the bathroom?	তুমি কি বাথরুমে যেতে চাও ?	[too-MEE KEE BAHT-room jeh-TAY CHAO]
Don't worry.	চিন্তা করো না।	[chin-TAH koh-ROH NAH]

Can I borrow that?	আমি কি এটা ধার করতে পারি ?	[ah mee oh-TAH dhahr kor-teh PAH-ree]
Excuse me.	মাপ করো / করুন।	[mahp KAW-roh/mahp koh-RUM]
Manners		
Please	দয়া করে…	[DAW-yah KOH-ray]
Thank you	ধন্যবাদ	[DON-noh-bahd]
Yes	হ্যাঁ	[hehn]
No	না	[nah]
May I?	আমি কি পারি ?	[ah-MEE KEE PAH-ree]
I'm sorry.	আমি দুঃখিত ?	[ah-MEE doo-KEE-toh]
Feelings		
Hungry	ক্ষুধার্ত	[khoo-DHAHR-toh]
Angry	রাগী / রাগত	[rah-GEE/rah-GAW-toh]
Lonely	একলা	[ack-LAH]
Tired	ক্লান্ত	[KLAHN-toh]
Thirsty	পিপাসিত	[pee-pah-shee-toh]
Sad	মন খারাপ	[mon KAH-rahp]
Happy	খুশী	[KOO-shee]
Worried	চিন্তিত	[chihn-TEE-toh]
Hurt	ব্যাথিত	[BA-tee-toh]
Commands/Requests		
Be quiet.	চুপ করো।	[choop KAW-roh]
Don't run.	দৌড়িও না।	[doh-REE-oh NAH]
Stop!	থামো!	[tah-MOH]
Line up.	লাইনে দাঁড়াও।	[lye-NAY dah-Rao]
Stand up.	উঠে দাঁড়াও।	[oo-TAY da-RAO]

English	Bengali	Pronunciation
Come here.	এখানে এসো।	[eh-KAH-nay eh-SHOH]
Point to…	…এর দিকে দেখাও।	[ehr DEE-kay, DA-kao]
Don't touch!	ছুঁয়ো না!	[CHOO-yoh nah]
I need help.	আমার সাহায্য লাগবে।	[ah-MAHR shah-hahj-JOH]
May I?	আমি কি করতে পারি?	[ah-MEE KOR-tay, PAH-ree]
Let's go!	চলো, আমরা যাই!	[CHAW-loh ,JAO-ah JAHK]
Raise your hand	হাত তোলো।	[HAHT toh-LOH]
Look	দেখো।	[dah-KOH]

Affirmations/Negations

English	Bengali	Pronunciation
Good!	ভালো!	[BHAH-loh]
Great work!	দারুণ কাজ!	[dah-ROON KAHJ]
That's better!	এবার ভালো হয়েছে!	[eh-BAHR b-hah-LOH hoh yek-CHEH]
O.K.	ঠিক আছে / আচ্ছা	[TEEK ah-CHAY]

School and Classroom Furnishings

English	Bengali	Pronunciation
Desk	ডেস্ক	Same as English
Chair	চেয়ার	[cheh-YAHR]
Table	টেবিল	Same as English
Chalkboard	ব্ল্যাকবোর্ড	Same as English
Flag	পতাকা	[paw-tah-KAH]
Door	দরজা	[DAWR-jah]
Window	জানালা	[JAHN-ah-lah]
Closet	ক্লজেট	Same as English
Trash can	ময়লার ঝুড়ি	Same as English
Hallway	করিডোর	Same as English
Office	অফিস / দপ্তর	Same as English
Boys'/Girls' Toilet	ছেলেদের/মেয়েদের বাথরুম	[cheh-leh-DEHR/meh-yeh-DEHR BAHT-room]
Gym	জিমনাসিয়াম	[JIHM-kah-nah]

English	Bengali	Pronunciation
Lunchroom	খাবার-ঘর	[kah-BAHR-gawp]
Pen	পেন / কলম	Same as English
Pencil	পেন্সিল	Same as English
Paper	কাগজ	[KAH-goj]
Tissue	টিস্যু কাগজ / টিস্যু	[mawch-HAHR KAH-goj]
Book	বই	[boi]
Shelf	তাক	[tahk]

School Activities

English	Bengali	Pronunciation
Homework	বাড়ির কাজ	Same as English
Test	পরীক্ষা	[paw-ree-KAH]
Report	রচনা	[raw-choh-NAH]
Study	পড়াশোনা	[paw-TAH-shoh-NAH]
Read	পড়া	[paw-RAH]
Write	লেখা	[leh-KAH]
Draw	আঁকা	[AHN-kah]
Listen	শোনা	[SHOH-nah]
Take this home to your parents.	এটা বাসায় তোমার মা-বাবা / অভিভাবক দেবে।	[ay-TAH bah-SHy TOH-mahr mah-bah-bah/ahb-BAH ahm-MAH-kay deh-BAY]

Chinese

English	Translation	Pronunciation
People		
I	我	[hnaw]
Me	我	[hnaw]
You	你	[nay]
You (plural)	你們	[NAY moon]
She	她	[tah]
He	他	[tah]
It	它	[tah]
We	我門	[HNAW moon]
Us	我門	[HNAW moon]
They	他門	[TAH moon]
Them	他門	[TAH moon]
My name is...	我的名字...	[hnaw DIHK mehng JEE]
Teacher	先生	[sihng SAHNG]
Student	學生	[hawk SAHNG]
Principal	校長	[HOW jehrng]
Parent	父母	[foo moh]
Mother	媽媽	[mah mah]
Father	爸爸	[bah BAH]
Sister	姊姊	[jee moi]
Brother	兄弟	[hihng DAI]
Parts of the Body		
Face	面	[meen]
Eye	眼	[hnahn]
Nose	鼻	[bay]
Mouth	口	[how]
Ear	耳	[yee]
Hand	手	[sow]
Finger	手指	[sow JEE]
Thumb	拇指	[moh JEE]
Arm	臂	[bay]
Leg	腿	[taw-ee]
Feet	足	[gehr]
Clothing, "body furniture"		
Hat	帽	[moh]
Glove	手套	[sow TOH]
Eyeglasses	眼鏡	[hnahn GEHNG]
Wheelchair	輪椅	[run YEE]
Braces (teeth and leg)	箍	[Koo]
Crutches	拐杖	[gwye jehrng]
Coat	外衣	[hnoi yee]
Sweater	冷衫	[moh YEE]
Shirt	恤衫	[yee]
Slacks (pants)	褲	[foo]
Shoes	鞋	[hye]
Socks	襪	[mutt]
Time		
Soon	將	[jehrng]
Now	現在	[yihn ZOI]
Later	遲一點	[chih SEH]
Today	今天	[gahm TEEN]
This morning	今早	[gahm JOH]
This afternoon	中午	[juhng mm]
Tonight	今晚	[gahm MAHN]

Yesterday	昨天	[jawk TEEN]
Tomorrow	明天	[mehng TEEN]

Place

Front	前	[chihn]
Back	後	[how]
Up	上	[sehrng]
Down	下	[hah]
On top	上面	[sehrng meen]
Underneath	下面	[HAH meen]
Here	在這裡	[joi jeh LOI]
There	在那裡	[joi hah LOI]
Inside	裡面	[LOI MEEN]
In	入	[yahp]
Out	出	[choot]
Left	左	[jaw]
Right	右	[yao]

Human Relations
Greetings, Goodbyes

Hello	好嗎	[hoh MAH]
Goodbye	再見	[Joy gihn]
Can I help?	可以幫你嗎？	[hoy yee BOHN nay mah]
I feel sick.	我覺得不舒服	[hnaw BEHN]
Help me.	幫我	[BAWNG hnaw]
I love you.	我愛你	[hnaw oi NAY]
Do you need to use the bathroom?	你要不要 用洗手間？	[Vay yew but yew yung sai sau gan]
Don't worry.	不要擔心	[baht yoo DAHM SUM]
Can I borrow that?	我可不可以借用	[Ngoh ho bat ho yi je na goh]
Excuse me.	原諒我	[yoo-ehn]

Manners

Please	請	[chehng]
Thank you	多謝	[DAW jay]
Yes	是	[see]
No	不是	[baht SEE]
May I?	可以嗎？	[haw YEE mah]
I'm sorry	對不起	[doi BAHT HAY]

Feelings

Hungry	飢餓	[gay hnoh]
Angry	怒	[noh]
Lonely	寂寞	[jihk mawk]
Tired	疲倦	[loi]
Thirsty	渴	[hawt]
Sad	傷心	[sow]
Happy	開心	[hoi SUM]
Worried	擔心	[DAHM sum]
Hurt	痛	[tawng]

Commands/Requests

Be quiet.	靜一靜	[zehng YAHT zehng]
Don't run.	不要跑	[baht yoo Zao]
Stop!	停	[tihng]
Line up.	排正	[pye doi]
Stand up.	起身	[hay SAHN]
Come here.	來	[loi]
Point to...	指向	[jee]
Don't touch!	不要摸	[baht yoo pehng]
I need help.	我要人幫助	[hnoh SOI yoo bawng joh]
May I?	我可以嗎？	[hoi yee MAH]

Let's go!	我們走吧！	[jao]
Raise your hand.	舉手	[goi sow]
Look.	看	[hawn]

Affirmations/Negations

Good!	好	[hoh]
Great work!	做得很	[JOH dahk HOH]
That's better!	好好多	[hoh dahk DOH]
O.K.	好	[hoh]

School and Classroom Furnishings

Desk	書桌	[seh JEE ɔi]
Chair	椅	[yee]
Table	餐桌	[toi]
Chalkboard	黑板	[hahk BAHN]
Flag	旗	[kay]
Door	門	[moon]
Window	窗	[chehrng]
Closet	衣櫃	[YEE choo]
Trash can	垃圾	[lye kahp]
Hallway	走廊	[JAO lon]
Office	辦公室	[bahn goong SAHT]
Boys'/Girls' Toilet	男／女洗手間	[Man/nui sai sau gaan]
Lunchroom	體育館	[mm CHΛHN goon]
Pen	筆	[baht]
Pencil	鉛筆	[yoo-chn BAHT]
Paper	紙	[JEE]
Tissue	紙巾	[choh JEE]
Book	書	[shoo]
Shelf	書	[shoo GΛH]

School Activities

Homework	功課	[GOONG faw]
Test	測驗	[CHAHT yihm]
Report	報告	[boh goh]
Study	學習	[wahn ZAHP]
Read	讀	[dawk]
Write	寫	[say]
Draw	畫	[wahk]
Listen	聽	[tehng]
Take this home to your parents.	拿回家給父母	[nah woo-ee GAH kahp FOO MOH]

Farsi

English	Translation		Pronunciation
People			
I	من		[man]
me	مرا - بمن		[ma-RAH/beh-MAN]
you	تو - تورا		[toh/toh-RAH]
you (plural)	شما - شمارا		[shoh-MAH/shoh-MAH-rah]
she	او (دختر)		[oo]
he	او (پسر)		[oo]
it	آن		[on]
we	ما		[mah]
us	ما را - بما		[mah-RAH/beh-MAH]
they	آنها		[ahn-HAH]
them	آنها را - به آنها		[ahn-HAH-rah/beh-ahn-HAH]
My name is...	نام من ...... است		[nah-MEH-man...ast]
Teacher	معلم		[moh-AH-lehm]
Student	محصل		[moh-HAH-sehl]
Principal	مدیر		[moh-DIHR]
Parent	پدر - مادر		[vaw-LEH-dayn]
Mother	مادر		[maw-DAHR]
Father	پدر		[peh-DAHR]
Sister	خواهر		[khaw-HAHR]
Brother	برادر		[ba-RAH-dahr]
Parts of the Body			
Face	صورت		[soo-rat]
Eye	چشم		[cheshm]
Nose	بینی		[bee-nee]
Mouth	دهان		[dah-HON]
Ear	گوش		[goosh]
Hand	دست		[dast]
Finger	انگشت		[ahn-GOHSHT]
Thumb	انگشت شست		[ahn-GOHSHT shast]
Arm	بازو		[baw-ZOO]
Leg	ساق پا		[paw]
Feet	پاها		[paw-HAH]
Clothing, "body furniture"			
Hat	کلاه		[koh-LAH]
Glove	دستکش		[dahst-KEHSH]
Eyeglasses	عینک		[AY-nak]
Wheelchair	ویلچر		Same as English
Braces (teeth and leg)	سیم (دهان و پا)		[seem]
Crutches	عصا		[ah-SAW]
Coat	کت		[Same as English]
Sweater	جلیقه		[JEH-lih-GAY]
Shirt	پیراهن		[pih-rah-HAHN]
Slacks (pants)	شلوار		[shal-VAHR]
Shoes	کفش		[kahfsh]
Socks	جوراب		[joo-RAHB]
Time			
Soon	زود		[zood]
Now	اکنون		[AK-noon]
Later	بعد		[BA-dahn]
Today	امروز		[EHM-rooz]
This morning	امروز صبح		[EHM-rooz SOB]
This afternoon	امروز بعد از ظهر		[EHM-rooz bah-dah-ZOOR]
Tonight	امشب		[EHM-shahb]

English	Farsi	Pronunciation
yesterday	دیروز	[dee-ROOZ]
tomorrow	فردا	[fahr-DAH]
Place		
front	جلو	[jeh-LOH]
back	عقب	[ah-GAHB]
up	بالا	[gah-lah]
down	پایین	[paw-een]
on top	روی	[roo-ee]
underneath	زیر	[zihr]
here	اینجا	[ihn-JAH]
there	آنجا	[ahn-JAH]
inside	داخل	[DAH-kehl]
in	در - داخل	[dahr/dah-KEHL]
out	بیرون	[bee-roon]
left	چپ	[chap]
right	راست	[rahst]
Human Relations		
Greetings, Goodbyes		
Hello	سلام	[sa-LAHM]
Goodbye	خداحافظ	[koh-DAH HAH-fehz]
Can I help?	من میتوانم کمک بکنم؟	[mee-tah-VAH-nam koh-MAK koh-NAM]
I feel sick.	حالم خوب نیست	[HAH-lam koob NEEST]
Help me.	بمن کمک کن	[beh koh-MAK kon]
I love you.	شما را دوست دارم	[shoh-MAH RAH doost DAH-ram]
Do you need to use the bathroom?	آیا به توالت احتیاج داری؟	[ah-YAH eh toh-vah-LEHT EH-TEE-ahj DAH-ree]
Don't worry.	نگران نباش	[nah-rah-FAT NAH-bosh]

English	Farsi	Pronunciation
Can I borrow that?	آیا من میتوانم آن را قرض کنم؟	[ah-YAH mee-TAH-vah-NAM ahn-RAH GAHRZ koh-NAM]
Excuse me.	ببخشید	[beh bahk SHEED]
Manners		
Please	لطفا	[loht-fan]
Thank you	متشکرم	[moh-tah-SHAH-keh-RAM]
yes	بله	[ba-LAY]
no	خیر	[na]
May I?	آیا من میتوانم؟	[ah-YAH mee-TAH-vah-nam]
I'm sorry.	متاسفم	[moh-TAH-seh-FAM]
Feelings		
Hungry	گرسنه	[goh-ROHS-nay]
Angry	عصبانی	[a-sah-BAW-nee]
Lonely	تنها	[tan-HAH]
Tired	خسته	[KAHS-tay]
Thirsty	تشنه	[tehsh-NAY]
Sad	غمگین	[gahm-geen]
Happy	شاد	[shod]
Worried	نگران	[neh-GAH-rahn]
Hurt	صدمه دیده	[SAH-dah-may dee-DAY]
Commands/Requests		
Be quiet.	ساکت باشید	[saw-KEHT baw-SHEED]
Don't run.	ندوید	[nah-DAH-reed]
Stop!	ایست	[eest]
Line up.	به صف بایستید	[beh SAHF beh-STEED]
Stand up.	بلند شوید	[boh-LAND shah-VEED]
Come here.	بیایید اینجا	[ihn-JAH bee-ah-IWD]

English	Farsi	Pronunciation
Gym	جيم (سالن ورزشي)	[Same as in English]
Lunchroom	سالن ناهارخوري	[nah-HAHR koh-REE]
Pen	قلم	[gah-LAM]
Pencil	مداد	[meh-DOD]
Paper	كاغذ	[kaw-GAZ]
Tissue	دستمال كاغذی	[DAHST-mahl KAW-gah-zee]
Book	كتاب	[keh-TAHB]
Shelf	قفسه	[gah-FAH-SEH]

School Activities

English	Farsi	Pronunciation
Homework	تكليف	[tak-LEEF]
Test	امتحان	[im-TAH-kahn]
Report	كارنامه	[KAHR-nah-meh]
Study	مطالعه	[MOH-tah-lay]
Read	بخوان	[beh-KAHN]
Write	بنويس	[beh-neh-VIHS]
Draw	بكش	[beh-KEHSH]
Listen	گوش كن	[GOOSH-kon]
Take this home to your parents.	اين را ببريد خانه برای پدر و مادرتان	[IN-rah beh-peh-DAHR vah maw-DAWR kohd dahr kah-NAY beh-BAH-rihd]

78

English	Farsi	Pronunciation
Point to...	به ...... اشاره كنيد	[beh...ESH-ah-RAY koh-NEED]
I need help.	من به كمك احتياج دارم	[beh koh-MAK EH-teh-AHJ dah-ram]
May I?	آيا ميتوانم؟	[ah-YAH MEE-tah vaw-NAM]
Let's go!	با برويم	[beh-RA-veem]
Raise your hand.	دستتان را بلند كنيد	[DAHS-teh-tahn-rah boh-LAND koh-Need]
Look.	نكاه كنيد	[neh-GAH koh-NEED]

Affirmations/Negations

English	Farsi	Pronunciation
Good!	خوب	[koob]
Great work!	آفرين	[AH-fah-reen]
That's better!	آن بهتر است	[ahn beh-FAHR ahsht]
O.K.	باشد	[baw-shad]

School and Classroom Furnishings

English	Farsi	Pronunciation
Desk	ميز	[meez]
Chair	صندلي	[san-dah-LEE]
Table	ميز (نيمكت)	[meez (nihm-KAT)]
Chalkboard	تخته سياه	[tahk-TEH SEE-aw]
Flag	پرچم	[ahr-chahm]
Door	در	[dahr]
Window	پنجره	[pan-JAH-reh]
Closet	كمد	[koh-mohd]
Trash can	آشغالدان	[ahsh-GAHL-dahn]
Hallway	راهرو	[rah-roh]
Office	اداره (دفتر)	[en-DAH-reh (dahf-TAHR)]
Boys'/Girls' Toilet	توالت دختر انه - پسرانه	[toh-VAH-leht dohk-TAH-rahm/peh-SAH-rahn]

Haitian-Creole

English	Translation	Pronunciation
People		
I	Pèp	[Pehp]
me	Mwen	[Mwehn]
You	Mwen	[Mwehn]
You (plural)	Yo	[Yoh]
She	Li	[Lee]
He	Li	[Lee]
It	Li	[Lee]
We	Nou	[Noo]
Us	Nou	[Noo]
They	Yo	[Yoh]
Them	Yo	[Yoh]
My name is...	Non Mwen se	[Naw Mwehn SAY]
Teacher	Pwofe sè	[Paw-feh-SAY]
Student	Elev	[Ay-lehv]
Principal	Principal	[Prihn-see-PAHL]
Parent	Paran	[Pah-rahn]
Mother	Manman	[Mah-Mah]
Father	Papa	[Pah-pah]
Sister	sè	[seh]
Brother	Frè	[Freh]
Parts of the Body		
Face	Figi	[FIH-gee]
Eye	Je	[Jay]
Nose	Nen	[Neh]
Mouth	Bouch	[Boosh]
Ear	Zorèy	[ZAW-ray]
Hand	Men	[Mehn]
Finger	Dwèt men	[DWEHT mehn]
Thumb	Pous	[Poos]
Arm	Bra	[Brah]
Leg	Kwis	[Kwihs]
Feet	Pie	[PEE-ay]
Clothing, "body furniture"		
Hat	Chapo	[SHAH-poh]
Glove	Gan	[Gahn]
Eyeglasses	Linèt	[Lee-NEHT]
Wheelchair	Chèz woulèt	[SHEHZ roo-LEHT]
Braces (teeth and leg)	Braslè (dan e kwis)	[BRAHS-lay (dhan eh kwees)]
Crutches	Beki (ba-kee)	[BEH-Kee]
Coat	Manto	[MAHN-toh]
Sweater	Chanday	[Shahn-DIE]
Shirt	Chemiz	[SHAY-meez]
Slacks (pants)	Pantalon	[PAHN-tah-lawn]
Shoes	Soulie	[soo-LEE-ay]
Socks	Chosèt	[Shoh-SHET]
Time		
Soon	Pita	[PEE-tah]
Now	Kounie-a	[KOH-nyay-ah]
Later	Pita	[PEE-tah]
Today	Jodi-a	[JOH-DEE-yah]
This morning	Matin-an	[MAH-tehn-ahn]
This afternoon	Aprè midi-a	[AH-pray mih-DEE-yah]

English	Creole	Pronunciation
Tonight	Asouè-a (aswè-a)	[AH-SWAY-yah]
Yesterday	Iè	[ee-yay]
Tomorrow	Demen	[DAY-mehn]

Place

English	Creole	Pronunciation
Front	Devan	[DAY-vahn]
Back	Dèiè	[DAY-ee-yay]
Up	An ho	[AHN hoh]
Down	An ba	[AHN ba]
On top	An lè tèt	[AHN ley THET]
Underneath	An ba	[AHN bah]
Here	Ici (isi)	[ee-SEE]
There	La	[Lah]
Inside	An n dan	[AHN dahn]
In	An n dan	[AHN dahn]
Out	Deyò	[DAY-yoh]
Left	Gòch	[Gohsh]
Right	Dwat	[Dwaht]

Human Relations
Greetings, Goodbyes

English	Creole	Pronunciation
Hello	Alo	[AH-lo]
Goodbye	Orevwa	[aw-RAY-vwah]
Can I help?	Mwen ka ede?	[MWEHN Kah eh-DAY]
I feel sick.	Mwen santi-m malad	[MWEHN sahn-TIHM MAH-lahd]
Help me.	Ede-m	[Ay-dehm]
I love you.	Mwen renmen-w	[Mwehn rehn-MAY OH]
Do you need to use the bathroom?	Eske ou vle itilize twaletla	[EHS-key OO vlay ih-tih-LEE-ZAY u twah-LEHT LAH]

English	Creole	Pronunciation
Don't worry.	Pa inkeyete-w	[PAH ehn-KEE-yeh-Tay-OH]
Can I borrow that?	Mwen ka prete sa-a	[MWEHN kah preh-TAY SAH-AH]
Excuse me.	Eskize-m	[EHS-Kee-Zeehm]

Manners

English	Creole	Pronunciation
Please	Si vou ple	[SIH voo paly]
Thank you	Mèsi	[MEH-See]
Yes	Wi	[wee]
No	NON	[Noh]
May I?	Mwen mèt?	[mwehn MEHT]
I'm sorry.	Mwen regrèt	[mwehn RAY-greht]

Feelings

English	Creole	Pronunciation
Hungry	Grangou	[GRAHN-goo]
Angry	Fache	[FAH-Shay]
Lonely	Sèl	[Sehl]
Tired	Fatige	[FAH-tee-gay]
Thirsty	Swaf	[Swahf]
Sad	Tris	[Trihs]
Happy	Kontan	[kwan-TAHN]
Worried	Inkyete	[ehn-KEE-yeh-TAY]
Hurt	Fèmal	[FAY-mahl]

Commands/Requests

English	Creole	Pronunciation
Be quiet.	Trankil	[Trahn-Kihl]
Don't run.	Pa kouri	[PAH Koo-ree]
Stop!	Kanpe!	[Kahn-pee]
Line up.	Kanpe nan ran	[Kahn-pee nahn rahn]
Stand up.	Kanpe	[Kahn-pee]
Come here.	Vini ici	[VIH-nee ih-SEE]

Haitian-Creole

English	Creole	Pronunciation
Point to...	Man-yen	[MAHN-yen]
Don't touch!	Pa man-yen	[PAH MAHN-yehn]
I need help.	Mwen bezwen ed	[mwehn be-ZWEHN EHD]
May I?	Posso?	[Poh-SOH]
Let's go!	An nou ale!	[ahn NOO ah-LEE]
Raise your hand.	Leve men ou	[leh-VAY MEHN-oo]
Look	Gade	[GAH-day]

Affirmations/Negations

English	Creole	Pronunciation
Good!	Bon!	[bahn]
Great work!	Bon travay	[bawn TRAH-vei]
That's better!	Se pibon!	[Say PEE-bohn]
O.K.	Oke	[Okay]

School and Classroom Furnishings

English	Creole	Pronunciation
Desk	Biwo	[BEE-woh]
Chair	Chèz	[Shehz]
Table	Tab	[tahb]
Chalkboard	Tablo	[tah-BLOH]
Flag	Drapo	[DRAH-poh]
Door	Pòt	[Pawt]
Window	Fenèt	[feh-NEHT]
Closet	Ti-chan-m	[tee shawn]
Trash can	Bokit fatra	[BOH-keht FAH-trah]
Hallway	Koulwa	[Kool-WAH]
Office	Ofis	[aw-FIHS]
Boys'/Girls' Toilet	Twalèt ti gason / tifi	[twah-LEHT tee GAH-sawn / tee fee]
Lunchroom	Sal-a-manje	[sahl-AH-MAHN-jay]
Pen	Plim	[plihm (pleem)]
Pencil	Kreyon	[KRAY-awn]

English	Creole	Pronunciation
Paper	Papye	[PAH-pyay]
Tissue	Papye twalèt	[PAH-pyay TWAH-leht]
Book	Liv (Leave)	[leev]
Shelf	Etajè	[EH-tah-jay]

School Activities

English	Creole	Pronunciation
Homework	Devwa	[day-VWAH]
Test	Ekzamen	[EHG-zah-mehn]
Report	Rapò	[RAH-poh]
Study	Etidye	[EH-tih-DYAY]
Read	Li (lee)	[lee]
Write	Ekri (A-Kree)	[EH-Kree]
Draw	Desen (DA-SIN)	[DAY-sihn]
Listen	Tande (TAN-DAY)	[TAHN-day]
Take this home to your parents.	Portalo a casa ai Pote sa-a lakay paran ou	[POHR-tah loh ah KAH-sah poh-TAY sah-ah lah-KIE PAH-rahn oo]

Hindi

English	Translation	Pronunciation
People		
I	मैं	[MAIN]
Me	मुझे	[MU-jhe]
You	तुम	[TU-m]
You (plural)	तुमलोग	[TUM-log]
She	वह	[WAH]
He	वह	[WAH]
It	यह	[YAH]
We	हमलोग	[hum-LOG]
Us	हमें	[HUM-en]
They	वे	[WAY]
Them	उन्हें	[UN-hen]
My name is...	मेरा नाम है	[mera-NAAM ... hai]
Teacher	शिक्षक	[SHIKCHHAK]
Student	विद्यार्थी	[vid-YAR-thi]
Principal	प्राचार्य	[PRA-char-ya]
Parent	माता – पिता	[maata-pita]
Mother	माता	[MA-ta]
Father	पिता	[PEE-ta]
Sister	बहन	[BA-HAN]
Brother	भाई	[b-hai]
Parts of the Body		
Face	चेहरा	[chai-hàRaa]
Eye	आँख	[AAK]
Nose	नाक	[NAAK]
Mouth	मुँह	[MU-han]
Ear	कान	[KAAN]
Hand	हाथ	[HAAT]
Finger	अँगुली	[ANG-guli]
Thumb	अंगूठा	[AN-gu-ta]
Arm	भुजा	[BHU-ja]
Leg	टांग	[TAA-ng]
Feet	पैर	[Ph-AIR]
Clothing, "body furniture"		
Hat	हैट	[HAT]
Glove	दस्ताना	[das-taNAA]
Eyeglasses	चश्मा	[shash-MAA]
Wheelchair	व्हील चेयर	[Wheelchair]
Braces (teeth and leg)	ब्रेसेज़ (टीथ पेंड लेग)	[Braces]
Crutches	बैशाखी	[way-SHA-key]
Coat	कोट	[Coat]
Sweater	स्वेटर	[Sweater]
Shirt	कमीज	[ka-mij]
Slacks (pants)	पतलून	[Pat-LOON]
Shoes	जूता	[JU-ta]
Socks	मोजा	[MO-ja]
Time		
Soon	जल्दी	[JAL-dee]
Now	अभी	[ABhee]
Later	बाद में	[BAAD-me]
Today	आज	[AAj]
This morning	आज सवह	[AAj Subha]
This afternoon	आज दोपहर	[CAAj-do-PAHER]
Tonight	आज रात	[Caaj RAAT]

Yesterday	कल	[KAL-h]
Tomorrow	कल	[KAL-h]

Place

Front	सामने	[SAAM-ne]
Back	पीछे	[PEE-che]
Up	ऊपर	[OOP-per]
Down	नीचे	[NEE-che]
On top	सबसे ऊपर	[Sab-se-OO=er]
Underneath	नीचे	[NEE-che]
Here	यहाँ	[YA-ha]
There	वहाँ	[Vah-HA]
Inside	अन्दर	[AAN-dar]
In	अन्दर	[AAN-der]
Out	बाहर	[BAA-her]
Left	बायें	[BAI-ye]
Right	दायें	[DAA-ye]

Human Relations
Greetings,Goodbyes

Hello	नमस्ते	[Hello]
Goodbye	नमस्कार	[NA-mas-kar]
Can I help?	क्या में मदद कर सकता हूँ ?	[Kya-mane-maddat-kar-SAKTA-whon]
I feel sick.	में बीमार हूँ	[May-bee-MAAR-whon]
Help me.	कृपया मदद करें	[KRIP-ya-MADAT-KARAY]
I love you.	में तुम से प्यार करता हूँ	[May-Tumse-PYAAR-Kar-ta-whon]
Do you need to use the bathroom?	क्या तुम्हें शौचालय जाना है ?	[Kya-TUM-hey Sauch-Al lay jana hay]
Don't worry.	चिंता मत करो	[Chinta-MAT-karo]

Can I borrow that?	क्या में वह ले सकता हूँ ?	[KYA MAIN WAH LE SAKTA HUN]
Excuse me.	मुझे क्षमा करो	[Muje Ksháma karo]

Manners

Please	कृपया	[KREE-paya]
Thank you	शुक्रिया धन्यवाद	[Shu-kriya Dhan-ya-baad]
Yes	हाँ	[Hah]
No	नहीं	[NA-HEE]
May I?	क्या में ?	[kya-may]
I'm sorry	में शर्मिन्दा हूँ	[may-shair-minda huhn]

Feelings

Hungry	भूख	[BHOO kha]
Angry	गुस्सा	[Gus-sa]
Lonely	अकेला	[AA-kela]
Tired	थका	[Tha-ka]
Thirsty	प्यासा	[Pya-asa]
Sad	दुखित	[Dook-hit]
Happy	खुश	[khuush]
Worried	चिन्तित	[chin-TIT]
Hurt	चोट	[chot]

Commands/Requests

Be quiet.	चुप रहो	[Chup RAHO]
Don't run.	मत भागो	[mat Bha-go]
Stop!	रुको	[Ru-ko]
Line up.	कतार में रहड़े हो	[KATAR may kha-re ho]
Stand up.	उठो	[OOT-ho]
Come here.	यहाँ आओ	[YAh-ha AO]

Pencil	पेन्सिल	[Pencil]
Paper	कागज	[KA-gaj]
Tissue	कागज की रुमाल	[KA-gaj Kiru-mal]
Book	किताब	[KEE-TAB]
Shelf	पटरी	[PAAT-RE]

School Activities

Homework	टास्क	[Task]
Test	परीक्षा	[PA-rik-sha]
Report	परीक्षा – फल	[PA-rik-sha phal]
Study	अध्ययन	[AAD-dhya-yam]
Read	पढ़ना	[Pad-ho]
Write	लिखना	[LIK-ho]
Draw	रिवंचना	[Khee-chana]
Listen	सुनो	[Soo-no]
Take this home to your parents.	यह अपने माता पिता के पास ले जाओ	[Ya apne MATTA-PITTA-PAASS-le-jaak]

84

Point to...	इशारा करो	[EE-shara karo]
Don't touch!	मत छुओ	[baht yoo pehng]
I need help.	मुझे मदद चाहिये	[MU-je madad CHA-EY]
May I?	क्या तुम ?	[Kya - MAIN]
Let's go!	चलो चलें	[CHE-lo CHA-len]
Raise your hand.	हाथ उठाओ	[HAAT-uthao]
Look.	देखो	[DEKH-ho]

Affirmations/Negations

Good!	अच्छा	[A-cha]
Great work!	शाबास	[SA-bash]
That's better!	वह अच्छा है	[wha A-ccha hay]
O.K.	ठीक है	[THEE-K hay]

School and Classroom Furnishings

Desk	मेज	[maize]
Chair	कुर्सी	[Kur-shee]
Table	मेज	[maize]
Chalkboard	ब्लेकबोर्ड	[Black board]
Flag	झंडा	[JHAN-da]
Door	दरवाजा	[dar-WA-ja]
Window	रिवड़की	[kir-KEE]
Closet	आलमारी	[AAL-maree]
Trash can	कूड़ादान	[KOO-RA dhan]
Hallway	बरामदा	[VâRANda]
Office	ऑफिस	[Office]
Boys'/Girls' Toilet	स्त्री / पुरुष शौचालय	[Sauch-cha-lay-IS-tree/Pu-roos]
Gym	व्यायामशाला	[VYA-yam-shala]
Lunchroom	भोजनकक्ष	[Bhoo-jan-kak-sha]
Pen	कलम	[KA-lam]

Italian

English	Translation	Pronunciation
People		
I	Io	[EE-oh]
Me	Io	[Meh]
You	Tu	[Tu]
You (plural)	Voi	[VOH-ee]
She	Lei	[la LEH-ee]
He	Lui	[la LUH-ee]
It	It	[el lah]
We	Noi	[NO-ee]
Us	Ci	[Chee]
They	Loro	[LOH-roh]
Them	Loro	[LOH-roh]
My name is...	Mi chiamo	[Mee KHIA-moh]
Teacher	Il maestro / la maestra	[Mah-EH-srtoh] / [Mah-EH-srah]
Student	Lo studente / la studentessa	[Stu-DEHN-teh] / [Stu-DEHN-teh-sah]
Principal	Il direttore	[Dee-reh-TOH-reh]
Parent	Il genitore	[Geh-nee-TOH-reh]
Mother	La madre	[MAH-dreh]
Father	Il padre	[PAH-dreh]
Sister	La sorella	[soh-reh-LAH]
Brother	Il fratello	[Frah-teh-LOH]
Parts of the Body		
Face	Il viso	[Vee-ZOH]
Eye	Gli occhi	[Oh-KEEY]
Nose	Il naso	[NAH-zoh]
Mouth	La bocca	[Boh-KAH]
Ear	Le orecchie	[Oh-rak-YEAH]
Hand	Le mani	[MAH-nee]
Finger	Le dita	[DEE-tah]
Thumb	Il pollice	[poh-LEE-cheh]
Arm	Le braccia	[Brah-CHA]
Leg	Le gambe	[GUM-beh]
Feet	I piedi	[PEE-a-dee]
Clothing, "body furniture"		
Hat	Il cappello	[Kah-PEH-loh]
Glove	I guanti	[WAN-tee]
Eyeglasses	Gli occhiali	[Oh-KIAH-lee]
Wheelchair	Sedia a rotelle	[SEH-Deeah Ah roh-teh-LEH]
Braces (teeth and leg)	L'Arco ortodontico	[Lah'AHR-koh Ohr-toh-dohn-TEE-koh]
Crutches	Le stampelle	[Stahn-PEH-leh]
Coat	Il cappotto	[Kah-POH-toh]
Sweater	La maglia	[Mahl-YAH]
Shirt	la camicia	[KAH-mee-cha]
Slacks (pants)	I pantaloni	[Pahn-TAH-loh-nee]
Shoes	Scarpe	[Skàrpe]
Socks	Calzini	[Kalzino]
Time		
Soon	Fra poco	[Frah POH-koh]
Now	Adeso	[Ah-DEH-soh]
Later	Dopo	[DOH-poh]
Today	Oggi	[OH-JEE]

English	Italian	Pronunciation
This morning	Stamattina	[Stah-mah-TEA-nah]
This afternoon	Questo pomeriggio	[KWE-stoh Poh-meh-JOH]
Tonight	Stasera	[Stah-SEH-rah]
Yesterday	Ieri	[YEAH-ree]
Tomorrow	Domani	[Doh-MAH-nee]

Place

English	Italian	Pronunciation
Front	Davanti	[Dah-VAHN-tee]
Back	Indietro	[EEN-de-eh-troh]
Up	Su	[Su]
Down	Giu'	[Juh]
On top	Sopra	[Soh-PRAH]
Underneath	Sotto	[Soh-TOH]
Here	Qua	[qui']
	Kwah'	[Kwee']
There	La	[Lah]
Inside	Interno	[Een-TEHR-noh]
In	Dentro	[Dehn-TROH]
Out	Fuori	[FUOH-ree]
Left	Sinistra	[See-NEE-strah]
Right	Destra	[Seh-STRAH]

Human Relations
Greetings, Goodbyes

English	Italian	Pronunciation
Hello	Buon giorno	[Buohn JOHR-noh]
Goodbye	Arrivederci	[Ah-REE-veh-dehr-chee]
Can I help?	Posso aiutare?	[Poh-SOH As-YOU-tah-reh]
I feel sick.	Mi siento male.	[Mee Sehn-TOH MAH-leh]
Help me.	Aiutami.	[Ah-YOU-tah-mee]
I love you.	Ti voglio bene.	[Tee VOH-glioh BEH-neh]

English	Italian	Pronunciation
Do you need to use the bathroom?	Devi andare in bagno?	[DEH-veh Ahn-DAH-reh een BAH-nyoh]
Don't worry.	Non ti preoccupare.	[Non Tee Preh-oh-KUH-pah-reh]
Can I borrow that?	Me lo presti?	[Mee loh PREH-sti]
Excuse me.	Scusami.	[SKUH-sah-mee]

Manners

English	Italian	Pronunciation
Please	Per favore	[Pehr FAH-voh-reh]
Thank you	Grazie	[GRAH-zyeah]
Yes	Si'	[See']
No	No	[Noh]
May I?	Posso?	[Poh-SOH]
I'm sorry.	Mi dispiace.	[Mee Dee-SPEEAH-che]

Feelings

English	Italian	Pronunciation
Hungry	Affamato/a	[Ah-FAH-mah-toh/tah]
Angry	arrabbiato/a	[Ah-RAH-biah-toh/tah]
Lonely	Solo/a	[SOH-loh/lah]
Tired	Stanco/a	[STAHN-koh/kah]
Thirsty	Assetato/a	[Ah-SEH-tah/toh/tah]
Sad	Triste	[TRI-steh]
Happy	Allegro/a	[As-LEH-groh/grah]
Worried	Preoccupato/a	[Preh-oh-KU-pah-toh/tah]
Hurt	Male	[mah-leh]

Commands/Requests

English	Italian	Pronunciation
Be quiet.	Stai zitto/a.	[Stah-EE ZEE-toh/tah]
Don't run.	Non correre.	[Nohn KOH-reh-reh]
Stop!	Fermati!	[FEHR-mah-tee]
Line up.	Allineati.	[Ahl-LEE-nee-ah-tee]

English	Italian	Pronunciation
Stand up.	Alzati.	[Ahl-ZAH-tee]
Come here.	Vieni qua.	[VIEH-nee kwah]
Point to...	Indica a...	[EEN-dee-kah Ah...]
Don't touch!	Non toccare!	[Nohn Toh-KAH-reh]
I need help.	Ho bisogno d'aiuto dah'.	[Oh bee-SOH-nyoh Ah-YOU-oh]
May I?	Posso?	[Poh-SOH]
Let's go?	Andiamo!	[AHN-diah-moh]
Raise your hand	Alza la mano.	[Ahl-zah lah MAH-noh]
Look	Guarda	[GUAHR-dah]

Affirmations/Negations

English	Italian	Pronunciation
Good!	Bene!	[BEH-neh]
Great work!	Ottimo Lavoro!	[OH-tee-moh LAH-voh-roh]
That's better!	Molto meglio!	[MOL-toh Meh-glioh]
O.K.	D'accordo	[Ah-KOR-doh]
	va bene	[Vah BEH-neh]

School and Classroom Furnishings

English	Italian	Pronunciation
Desk	La scrivania	[SKREE-vah-nee-ah]
Chair	La sedia	[SEH-dee-ah]
Table	Il tavolo	[TAH-voh-loh]
Chalkboard	La lavagna	[Lah-VAH-nyah]
Flag	La bandiera	[BAHN-cee-ah-rah]
Door	La porta	[POHR-tah]
Window	La finestra	[Fee-NEH-strah]
Closet	Il guardaroba	[WHAR-dah roh-bah]
Trash can	La pattumiera	[Pah-TU-I-mee-ah-rah]
Hallway	Il corridoio	[Koh-REE-doh-yoh]
Office	L'ufficio	[Uh-FEE-cho]

English	Italian	Pronunciation
Boys'/Girls' Toilet	La toletta/uomo/moh/	[Toh-leh-tah/UOH-donna DOH-nah]
Gym	La palestra	[Pah-LEH-strah]
Lunchroom	La tavola calda	[TAH-voh-lah KAL-dah]
Pen	La penna	[PEH-nah]
Pencil	La matita	[MAH-tee-tah]
Paper	La carta	[KAR-tah]
Tissue	Fazzoletti di carta	[Fah-ZOH-leh-tee dee KAR-tah]
Book	I libri	[LEE-bree]
Shelf	I scaffali	[Skah-FAH-lee]

School Activities

English	Italian	Pronunciation
Homework	I compiti	[KOM-pee-tee]
Test	L'esame	[Eh-SAH-meh]
Report	Ricerca	[Rich]
Study	Studiare	[STU-dee-ah-reh]
Read	Leggere	[LEH-geh-reh]
Write	Scrivere	[SKREE-veh-reh]
Draw	Disegnare	[Dee-seh-NYAH-reh]
Listen	Ascoltare	[Ah-SKOL-tah-reh]
Take this home to your parents.	Portalo a casa ai tuoi genitori.	[POHR-tah loh ah KAH-sah AH-ee Tuo-ee geh-nee-TOH-ree]

Korean

English	Translation	Pronunciation
People		
I	나	[Nah]
me	나에게	[Nah eh keh]
you	당신	[Dahng shin]
you (plural)	당신들	[Dahng shin deul]
she	그 여자	[Kuh yuh chah]
he	그 남자	[Kuh nahm chah]
it	그것	[Kuh koht]
we	우리	[Woo rih]
us	우리들	[Woo rih deul]
they	그들	[Kue deul]
them	그들	[Kue deul]
My name is...	나의 이름은...	[Nah ui ee reum eun]
Teacher	선생	[Suhn sang]
Student	학생	[Hahk sang]
Principal	교장	[Kyo jahng]
Parent	부모	[Boo moh]
Mother	어머니	[Uh muh nih]
Father	아버지	[Ah buh ji]
Sister	자매	[Cha mah]
Brother	형제	[Hyung jae]
Parts of the Body		
face	얼굴	[Uhl gool]
eye	눈	[Noon]
nose	코	[Koh]
mouth	입	[Ip]
ear	귀	[Kui]
hand	손	[Sohn]
finger	손가락	[Sohn gah rahk]
thumb	엄지 손가락	[Uhm ji sohn gah rahk]
arm	팔	[Pahl]
leg	다리	[Dah ri]
feet	발	[Bahl]
Clothing, "body furniture"		
hat	모자	[Moh jah]
glove	장갑	[Chang gahb]
eyeglasses	안경	[Ahn kyong]
wheelchair	휠체어	[Wheel chair]
braces (teeth and leg)	치열 교정기	[Chi yol kyo jung kih]
	버팀대	[Buh teem dae]
crutches	목다리	[Moh dah rih]
coat	코트	[coat]
sweater	스웨터	[Sweater]
shirt	샤쓰	[Shirts]
slacks (pants)	바지	[Bah ji]
shoes	신발	[Shin bahl]
socks	양말	[Yang Mahl]
Time		
soon	곧	[Goht]
now	지금	[Chi Keum]
later	후에	[Whoo eh]
not yet	아직	[Ah jik]
today	오늘	[Oh nuel]
this morning	오늘 아침	[Oh nuel ah chim]

Korean

Do you need to use the bathroom?	화장실에 가셔야 됩니까?	[Hwa chang shil eh gah yah dep ni kkah]
Don't worry.	걱정하지 마세요	[Kok jung hah ji ma seh yo]
Can I borrow that?	그 것을 빌릴 수 있을까요?	[Kue goht eul bil lil soo kkah yo]
Excuse me.	실례합니다	[Shil lyeh hahm ni tah]

Manners

Please	제발	[Che bahl]
Thank you	감사합니다	[Kam sah hahm ni tah]
yes	네	[Nyeh]
no	아니오.	[Ah ni yo]
May I?	내가 …해도 될까요?	[Nah kah …ha doh doel kkah yo]
I'm sorry	미안 합니다.	[Mi ahn ham ni tah]

Feelings

Hungry	배고픈	[Bae go poon]
Angry	화난	[Hwa nahn]
Lonely	외로운	[Wei roh woon]
Tired	피곤한	[Pi gohn hahn]
Thirsty	목마른	[Mohk mah reun]
Sad	슬픈	[Seul poon]
Happy	행복한	[Hang bohk hahn]
Worried	걱정된	[Kohk chong dwen]
Hurt	아픈	[Ah poon]

Commands/Requests

Be quiet.	조용히 해	[Cho yong hee hah]
Don't run.	뛰지 마십시오	[Ddui chi mah shib si yo]
Stop!	정지!	[Chong chi]

this afternoon	오늘 오후	[Oh neul oh too]
tonight	오늘 밤	[Oh nuel bahm]
yesterday	어제	[Uh jeh]
tomorrow	내일	[Nah il]

Place

front	앞	[Ahp]
back	뒤	[Dui]
up	위	[Ui]
down	아래	[Ah rae]
on top	꼭대기	[Kkok Dde gi]
underneath	밑	[Mit]
here	여기	[Yoh gi]
there	저기	[Joh gi]
inside	내부	[Nah boo]
in	안	[Ahn]
out	밖	[Pahk]
left	왼쪽	[When jjok]
right	오른쪽	[Oh reun jjok]

Human Relations
Greetings, Goodbyes

Hello	여보세요	[Yuh boh seh yo]
Goodbye	안녕	[Ahn nyung]
Can I help?	도와 드릴까요?	[Doh wah due ril kkah yo]
I feel sick.	아픈것 같읍니다	[Ah poon guht got ssuem dah]
Help me.	도와 주십시오	[Do wha joo sip sih yo]
I love you.	당신을 사랑합니다	[Dahn shin eul sah rang hahm ni dah]

Boys'/Girls' Toilet	남자용 화장실	[Nahm jah yong hwa chang shil]
	여자용 화장실	[Yuh jah yong hwa chang shil]
Gym	체육관	[Che yook kwan]
Lunchroom	식당	[Shik dahng]
Pen	펜	[Pen]
Pencil	연필	[Yun pil]
Paper	종이	[Chong ee]
Tissue	화장지	[Hwa chang chi]
Book	책	[Chak]
Shelf	선반	[Suhn bahn]

School Activities

Homework	숙제	[Sook cheh]
Test	시험	[Shi hum]
Report	보고서	=[Bo go suh]
Study	공부	[Gohng boo]
Read	읽다	[Eel tah]
Write	쓰다	[Sseu tah]
Draw	그리다	[Keu rih tah]
Listen	듣다	[Deut tah]
Take this home to your parents	이것을 부모님 한테 갖다 주십시요	[ee guht eul boo moh nim hahn teh goht tah joo ship si yo]

Line up.	줄 서십시오	[Jool soh shib si yo]
Stand up.	일어 서십시오	[Il oh shib shib si yo]
Come here.	이리 오십시오	[Ee ri oh shib si yo]
Point to...	...지적 하라	[...chi joh hah rah]
Don't touch!	만지지 마세요	[Mahn chi chi mah seh yo]
I need help.	도와 주십시오	[Do wha joo sip sih yo]
May I?	내가 ...해도 될까요?	[Nah kah ...ha doh doel kkah yo?]
Let's go!	갑시다	[Kab shi tah]
Raise your hand.	손을 드세요	[Sohn eul deu seh yo]
Look.	보아라	[Boh ah rah]

Affirmations/Negations

Good!	좋다	[Chot tah!]
Great work!	잘했어!	[Chol hat suh!]
That's better!	그것이 더 좋다	[Geu got ee doh chot tah]
O.K.	좋다	[Chot tah]

School and Classroom Furnishings

Desk	책상	[Chak sahng]
Chair	의자	[Ui cha]
Table	상	[Sahng]
Chalkboard	칠판	[Chil pahn]
Flag	국기	[Kook kih]
Door	문	[Moon]
Window	창문	[Chang moon]
Closet	옷장	[Oht chang]
Trash can	쓰레기 통	[Sseu reh ki tong]
Hallway	복도	[Bok doh]
Office	사무실	[Sah moo shil]

Polish

English	Translation	Pronunciation
People		
I	Ja	[yah]
Me	Mnie	[mnyeh]
You	Ty	[teh]
You (plural)	Wy	[veh]
She	Ona	[oh-NAH]
He	On	[on]
It	Ono	[oh-NOH]
We	My	[meh]
Us	Nas	[nahs]
They	Oni	[oh-NEE]
Them	Oni	[oh-NEE]
My name is...	Nazywam się	[nah-ZEH-vam sheh]
Teacher	Profesor	[pro-FES-or]
Student	Student	[stoo-DEHNT]
Principal	Dyrektor	[deh-RAHK-tuhr]
Parent	Rodzice	[ro-JEETZ-eh]
Mother	Matka	[mat-KAH]
Father	Ojciec	[oj-CHETZ]
Sister	Siostra	[show-STRAH]
Brother	Brat	[braht]
Parts of the Body		
Face	twarz	[tvash]
Eye	oczy	[oh-CHEH]
Nose	nos	[nos]
Mouth	usta	[oo-STAH]
Ear	ucho	[oo-KHOH]
Hand	ręka	[reh-KAH]
Finger	palec	[pah-LETS]
Thumb	kciuk	[ktchook]
Arm	ciało	[cha-WOH]
Leg	noga	[noh-GAH]
Feet	stopa	[stoh-PAH]
Clothing, "body furniture"		
Hat	kapelusz	[kha-PEL-oosh]
Glove	rekawiczki	[re-kav-EETCH-kee]
Eyeglasses	okulary	[oh-koo-LAH-reh]
Wheelchair	wózek inwalidzki	[vro-ZHEK een-vah-LEEDTZ-kee]
Braces (teeth and leg)	klamra	[klah-MRAH]
Crutches	kule inwalidzkie	[kooh-LEH in-vah-LEEDTZ-kee]
Coat	płaszcz	[pwashch]
Sweater	sweter	[SVER-tehr]
Shirt	koszula	[koh-SHOO-lah]
Slacks (pants)	spodnie	[SPOD-nyeh]
Shoes	buty	[BOO-teh]
Socks	skarpety	[skar-PHE-teh]
Time		
Soon	wkrótce	[VKROOHT-seh]
Now	teraz	[TEH-rasz]
Later	później	[poosh-NEE-yehy]
Today	dzisiaj	[JEE-shy]
This morning	rano	[RA-noh]

English	Polish	Pronunciation
This afternoon	popołudnie	[poh-poh-WOOD-nyeh]
Tonight	wieczorem	[vyeh-CHOR-em]
Yesterday	wczoraj	[vchoh-RAIY]
Tomorrow	jutro	[yoo-TROH]

Place

English	Polish	Pronunciation
Front	przód	[pzhod]
Back	tył	[tehw]
Up	góra	[GOH-rah]
Down	dół	[DOH-leh]
On top	na górze	[na GOR-sheh]
Underneath	pod spodem	[pohd SPUH-dem]
Here	tu	[too]
There	tam	[tahm]
Inside	wnętrze	[VNOUN-sheh]
In	w	[veh]
Out	precz	[pretch]
Left	lewo	[LEH-voh]
Right	prawo	[PRAH-voh]

Human Relations
Greetings, Goodbyes

English	Polish	Pronunciation
Hello	Hallo	[HAH-loh]
Goodbye	Dowidzenia	[doh-veed-ZEN-ya]h]
Can I help?	Ja ci pomogę	[yah chee poh-MEH-geh]
I feel sick.	Ja się źle czuję	[yah sheh zley CHOO-yeh]
Help me.	Pomóż mi	[POH-moosh mee]
I love you.	Kocham cię	[KOH-ham-cheh]
Do you need to use the bathroom?	Czy ty chcesz wyjść do ubikacji	[cheh teh ksesh vyeesht doh ooh-bee-KAHT-se]
Don't worry.	Nie martwsię	[nyeh MART-veh]

English	Polish	Pronunciation
Can I borrow that?	Ja ci pożyczę	[yah cee poz-SHECH-eh]
Excuse me.	Przepraszam	[psheh-PRAH-sham]

Manners

English	Polish	Pronunciation
Please	Proszę	[PROH-sheh]
Thank you	Dziekuję	[gin-KOO-yeh]
Yes	Tak	[tahk]
No	Nie	[nyeh]
May I?	Czy mogę	[cheh MOH-geh]
I'm sorry	Przepraszam	[psheh-PRAH-sham]

Feelings

English	Polish	Pronunciation
Hungry	głodny	[GWUD-neh]
Angry	zły	[zweh]
Lonely	samotny	[sahm-MOTT-neh]
Tired	zmęczony	[zmoun-CHOH-neh]
Thirsty	spragniony	[spran-NYOH-neh]
Sad	smutny	[SMOOT-neh]
Happy	szczęśliwy	[shcheh-SHLEE-veh]
Worried	zdenerowany	[zoh-leh-neh-roh-VAH-neh]
Hurt	uderzony	[oo-deh-ZHOH-neh]

Commands/Requests

English	Polish	Pronunciation
Be quiet.	Cicho	[CHEE-hoh]
Don't run.	Nie biegiaj	[nyeh BYEH-guy]
Stop!	Stój	[stoy]
Line up.	Stań w szeregu	[stahn veh sheh-REH-goo]
Stand up.	Wstań	[vstahn]
Come here.	Chodz tu	[hutch too]
Point to...	Pokazać	[pu-KAZ-atch]
Don't touch!	Nie dotykaj	[nyeh doh-TEH-kay]

I need help.	Pomóż mi	[Poh-MUHTS mee]
May I?	Czy mogę	[cheh MOH-geh]
Let's go?	Idz	[eetch]
Raise your hand.	Podnieś rękę	[puhd-NYESH reh-KEH]
Look.	Popatrz	[POH-patzh]

Affirmations/Negations

Good!	Dobry!	[DOH-breh]
Great work!	Dobrze zrobione!	[DOHB-zheh zrow-BEEYOH-neh]
That's better!	To jest lepsze!	[toh yest LEP-sheh]
O.K.	Dobrze	[DOHB-zhen]

School and Classroom Furnishings

Desk	biurko	[BEEYOR-koh]
Chair	kreslo	[KZHEH-swoh]
Table	stół	[stoow]
Chalkboard	tablica	[tab-LEET-sah]
Flag	Flaga	[FLAH-gah]
Door	Drzwi	[dzhevee]
Window	Okno	[OHK-noh]
Closet	Szafa	[SHAH-fah]
Trash can	Śmietnik	[shmyeht-NEEK]
Hallway	Hol	[huhl]
Office	Biuro	[OH-fees]
Boys'/Girls' Toilet	Damskä Meska Toaleta	[DAHM-skah, MOUN-ska toh-ah-LEH-tah]
Gym	Sala gimnastyczna	[SAH-lah jeem-nah-STYCH-nah]
Lunchroom	Kuchnia	[KUKH-nyah]
Pen	Pioro	[pyor-OH]

Pencil	Olowek	[oh-WOH-vek]
Paper	Papier	[pah-PEE-yer]
Tissue	Chusteczka	[hoos-TETCH-kah]
Book	Książka	[KSHOUN-shkah]
Shelf	Półka	[poow-KAH]

School Activities

Homework	Praca domowa	[doh-MOH-va PRA-sah]
Test	Test	[tehst]
Report	Sprawozdanie	[sprah-voz-DAH-nyah]
Study	Uczyć się	[OO-chich sheh]
Read	Czytać	[CHEH-tye]
Write	Piać	[peesh]
Draw	Rysować	[reh-SUHYEE]
Listen	Słuchać	[SWOOH-hi]
Take this home to your parents.	Weź do domu dla swoich rodziców.	[vesh doh doh-MOO dlah sfoyk rod JEET soovdrehz]

Russian

English	Translation	Pronunciation
People		
I	Я	[yah]
Me	Мне	[mnyeh]
You	Ты	[ty]
You (plural)	Вы	[vy]
She	Она	[ah-NAW]
He	Он	[awn]
It	Оно	[awn-NUH]
We	Мы	[my]
Us	Нас	[HUM-en]
They	Они	[ah-NEE]
Them	Им	[eem]
My name is...	Меня зовут...	[mee-NYAH zah-VOOT]
Teacher	Учитель	[oo-CHEE-teel']
Student	Студент/ученик	[stoo-DYEHNT]
Principal	Директор	[dee-REHK-tuhr]
Parent	Родитель	[rah-DEET-eel']
Mother	Мать	[maht']
Father	Отец	[ah-TYEHTS]
Sister	Сестра	[see-STRAH]
Brother	брат	[braht]
Parts of the Body		
Face	лицо	[lee-TSAW]
Eye	глаз	[glahs]
Nose	нос	[naws]
Mouth	рот	[rawt]
Ear	ухо	[OO-khuh]
Hand	рука	[roo-KAH]
Finger	палец	[PAH-leets]
Thumb	большой палец	[bahl'-SHOY PAH-leets]
Arm	рука	[nah-GAH]
Leg	нога	[nah-GAH]
Feet	ноги	[Ph-AIR]
Clothing, "body furniture"		
Hat	шапка	[SHAHP-kuh]
Glove	перчатка	[peer-CHAHT-kuh]
Eyeglasses	очки	[ahch-KEE]
Wheelchair	инвалидная коляска	[een-vah-LEED-nuh-yuh kah-LYAHS-kuh]
Braces (teeth and leg)	пластинка для исправления зубов/шина	[pla-STIN-ka dlya isprav-LE-niya zu-BOV/SHI-na]
Crutches	костыли	[kahs-ty-LYEE]
Coat	пальто	[pahl'-TAW]
Sweater	свитер	[SVEE-teer]
Shirt	рубашка	[roo-BAHSH-kuh]
Slacks (pants)	брюки	[BRYOO-kee]
Shoes	туфли	[AW-boof; TOOf-lee]
Socks	носки	[nahs-KEE]
Time		
Soon	скоро	[SKAW-ruh]
Now	сейчас	[syee-CHAHS]
Later	позже	[PAW-zheh]
Today	сегодня	[see-VAWD-nyuh]

English	Russian	Pronunciation
This morning	УТРОМ	[OO-truhm]
This afternoon	ДНёМ	[dnyawm]
Tonight	ВЕЧЕРОМ	[VYEH-chee-ruhm]
Yesterday	ВЧЕРА	[fchee-RAH]
Tomorrow	ЗАВТРА	[ZAHF-truh]

Place

English	Russian	Pronunciation
Front	ВПЕРЕДИ	[fpee-ree-DEE]
Back	СЗАДИ	[ZAH-dee]
Up	ВВЕРХ	[vyehrkh]
Down	ВНИЗ	[vnees]
On top	СВЕРХУ	[SVYEHR-khoo]
Underneath	ВНИЗУ	[vnee-ZOO]
Here	ТУТ, ВОТ, ЗДЕСЬ	[toot; vawt zdyehs']
There	ТАМ	[vah HA]
Inside	ВНУТРИ	[vnoo-TREE]
In	В	[v]
Out	ВНЕ	[vnyeh]
Left	СЛЕВА	[SLYEH-vuh]
Right	СПРАВА	[SPRAH-vuh]

Human Relations
Greetings, Goodbyes

English	Russian	Pronunciation
Hello	ЗДРАВСТВУЙТЕ	[ZDRAH-stvooy-tyeh!]
Goodbye	ДО СВИДАНИЯ	[dah svee-DAH-nee-yuh]
Can I help?	Я МОГУ ПОМОЧЬ?	[yah BAW-leen/bahl'NAH]
I feel sick.	Я плохо себя чувствую.	[yah BAW-leen/bahl'Nah]
Help me.	Помогите мне.	[mnyeh!]
I love you.	Я вас люблю.	[yah vahs lyoo-BLOO.]

English	Russian	Pronunciation
Do you need to use the bathroom?	Вам нужно в туалет?	[vahm NOOZH-nuh f too-ah-LYEHT]
Don't worry.	Не волнуйтесь	[nyeh vahl-NOOY-tees']
Can I borrow that?	Можно одолжить?	[MAWZH-nuh ah-dahl-ZHYT']
Excuse me.	Извините.	[ee-zvee-NEE-tyeh.]

Manners

English	Russian	Pronunciation
Please	Пожалуйста	[pah-ZHAHL-stuh]
Thank you	Спасибо	[spah-SEE-buh]
Yes	да	[dah]
No	нет	[nyeht]
May I?	Можно?	[MAWZH-nuh?]
I'm sorry	Простите.	[prah-STEE-tyeh.]

Feelings

English	Russian	Pronunciation
Hungry	Голодный	[gah-LAED-ny]
Angry	Злой	[zlawy]
Lonely	Одинокий	[ah-dee-NAW-kee]
Tired	Уставший	[oos-TAHV-shy]
Thirsty	я хочу пить	[khah-CHOO peet']
Sad	Печальный	[pee-CHAHL'-nuh]
Happy	Счастливый	[SHAST-lee-vy]
Worried	Обеспокоенный	[ah-bees-pah-KAW-yeen-ny]
Hurt	Обиженный	[bah-LEHZ-neen-ny]

Commands/Requests

English	Russian	Pronunciation
Be quiet.	Тихо	[TEE-kho]
Don't run.	Не бегите	[nee bee-GEE-tee]
Stop!	Остановитесь!	[ah-stah-nah-VEE-tyees']

English	Russian	Pronunciation
Line up.	Встаньте в очередь.	[VS'THN'-tyeh v AW-chee-reed']
Stand up.	Встаньте.	[VSTAN'-tyeh]
Come here.	Идите сюда.	[[ee-TEE syoo-DAH.]
Point to…	Укажите…	[oo-kah-ZHEE-tyeh]
Don't touch!	Не трогайте!	[nyeh TRAW-guhy-teh]
I need help.	Помогите мне.	[puh-mah-GEE-tyeh mnyeh.]
May I?	Можно?	[MAWZH-nuh?]
Let's go!	Пошли!	[pahsh-LEE!]
Raise your hand.	Поднимите руку.	[puhd-nee-MEE-teh ROO-koo.]
Look.	Смотри	[smah-TREHYEE].

Affirmations/Negations

English	Russian	Pronunciation
Good!	Хорошо!	[[khah-rah-SHAW!]
Great work!	Хорошая работа!	[khah-RAW-shuh-yah rah-BAW-tah!]
That's better!	Это лучше!	[EH-tuh Loo-cheh!]
O.K.	Хорошо.	[khah-rah-SHAW]

School and Classroom Furnishings

English	Russian	Pronunciation
Desk	Стол	[stawl]
Chair	Стул	[stool]
Table	Стол	[stawl]
Chalkboard	Доска	[dahs-KAH]
Flag	Флаг	[flahg]
Door	Дверь	[dveer']
Window	Окно	[ahk-NAW]
Closet	Стенной шкаф	[stee-NOY shkahf]
Trash can	Мусорное ведро	[MOO-shur-nuh-yeh vee-DRAW]

English	Russian	Pronunciation
Hallway	коридор	[kah-ree-DAWR]
Office	контора	[kahn-TAW-ruh]
Boys'/Girls' Toilet	Туалет для маль-чиков /для девочек	[too-ah-LYEHT/dlyah DYEH-vuh-cheek/MAHL'-cheek-kuhv/]
Gym	Спортивный зал	[spahr-TEEV-ny zahl]
Lunchroom	Столовая	[stah-LAWV-uh-yuh]
Pen	Ручка	[ROOCH-kuh]
Pencil	Карандаш	[kah-rahn-DAHSH]
Paper	Бумага	[boo-MAH-guh]
Tissue	Бумажная салфетка	[boo-MAHZH-nuh-yuh sahl-FYEHT-kuh]
Book	Книга	[KNEE-guh]
Shelf	Полка	[PAWL-kuh]

School Activities

English	Russian	Pronunciation
Homework	Домашняя работа	[da-MAHSH-neeh-yuh rah-BAW-tuh]
Test	Контрольная работа	[kahn-TRAWL'-nuh-yuh rah-BAW-tuh]
Report	Докладывать	[dah-KLAH-dy-vaht']
Study	Изучать	[ee-ZOO-chaht']
Read	Читать	[chee-TAHT']
Write	Писать	[pee-SAHT']
Draw	Рисовать	[ree-sah-VAHT']
Listen	Слушать	[SLOO-shuht']
Take this home to your parents .	Отнесите это своим родителям	[aht-nee-SEE-tyeh EH-tah rah-dee-tee-LYAHM]

Serbo-Croatian

English	Translation	Pronunciation
People		
I	Ja	[yah]
Me	Mene	[MEN-eh]
You	Ti	[tee]
You (plural)	Vi	[vee]
She	Ona	[OH-na]
He	On	[on]
It	Ono	[OH-noh]
We	Mi	[mee]
Us	Nas	[nahs]
They	Oni	[OH-nee]
Them	Njih	[nyee-h]
My name is...	Moje ime je...	[MO-yeh EE-meh yeh]
Teacher	Ucitelj	[OOCH-eh-tehl]
Student	Ucenik	[OOCH-eh-nihck]
Principal	Direktor skole	[dih-REHCK- tor SHKOL-eh]
Parent	Roditelj	[RAW-deh-tehl-yeh]
Mother	Majka	[MY-kah]
Father	Otac	[OH-tahtz]
Sister	Sestra	[SEHS-trah]
Brother	Brat	[braht]
Parts of the Body		
Face	Lice	[LEE-tzeh]
Eye	Oko	[oh-koh]
Nose	Nos	[naws]
Mouth	Usta	[OO-stah]
Ear	Uho	[OO-haw]
Hand	Saka	[SHAH-kah]
Finger	Prst	[purst]
Thumb	Palac	[PAHL-ahtz]
Arm	Ruka	[ROO-kah]
Leg	Noga	[noh-gah]
Feet	Stopalo	[STOH-pah-loh]
Clothing, "body furniture"		
Hat	Kapa	[kah-pah]
Glove	Rukavica	[roo-kah-VEE-tzah]
Eyeglasses	Naocale	[NAO-OH-chah-leh]
Wheelchair	Invalidska kolica	[in-vah-LEED-skah koh-LEE-tzah]
Braces (teeth and leg)	Proteza za (zube i nog)	[proh-TAY-ZAH za (zoo-beh-ee noh-goo)]
Crutches	Stake	[SHTAH-keh]
Coat	Kaput	[CAH-poot]
Sweater	Vesta	[ves-tah]
Shirt	Kosulja	[KOHSH-ool-yah]
Slacks (pants)	Hilace	[hil-ACH-eh]
Shoes	Cipele	[TZEE-peh-leh]
Socks	Carape	[chah-RAHP-EH]
Time		
Soon	Uskoro	[OOS-kaw-roh]
Now	Sada	[sah-dah]
Later	Kasnije	[KAHS-nee-yeh]
Today	Danas	[dahn-nahs]
This morning	Jutros	[yoo-tros]

This afternoon	Popodne	[dah-nahs poh-POD-neh]
Tonight	Veceras	[vetch-AIR-ehs]
Yesterday	Jucer	[yoo-chehr]
Tomorrow	Sutra	[soo-trah]

Place

Front	Ispred	[IS-prehd]
Back	Iza	[EE-zah]
Up	Gore	[gaw-reh]
Down	Dolje	[DOHL-yeh]
On top	Na vrhu	[nah VEHR-HOO]
Underneath	Ispod	[is-pod]
Here	Ovdje	[ov-DEE-ay]
There	Tamo	[tah-moh]
Inside	Iznutra	[iz-noo-TRAH]
In	U	[oo]
Out	Izvan	[iz-vahn]
Left	Lejevo	[LEH-ih-voh]
Right	Desno	[DEHS-noh]

Human Relations
Greetings, Goodbyes

Hello	Zdravo	[zeh-DRAH-voh]
Goodbye	Dovidjenja	[doh-VEED-JAYN-yah]
Can I help?	Da li mogu pomoci?	[DAH LEE maw-goo paw-maw-CHEE]
I feel sick.	Ne osjecam se dobro.	[neh oh-SEE-ay-CHUM seh doh-BRAW]
Help me.	Pomozi mi.	[poh-MAW-ZEE mee]
I love you.	Volim te.	[voh-LIHM teh]

Do you need to use the bathroom?	Da li treabte ici na zahod?	[DAH LEE tray-bah-teh ee-chee nah zah-HOHT]
Don't worry.	Ne brini.	[NEH bree-nee]
Can I borrow that?	Da li mogu to posuditi?	[DAH LEE moh-goo toh poh-soo-dih-TEE]
Excuse me.	Izvinite.	[ihz-veen-ee-teh]

Manners

Please	Molim	[maw-lihm]
Thank you	Hvala	[HEHR-ah-lah]
Yes	Da	[dah]
No	Ne	[heh]
May I?	Da li mogü?	[DAH-LEE moh-goo]
I'm sorry	Zao mi je	[JAO mee yeh]

Feelings

Hungry	Gladan	[GLAH-dahn]
Angry	Ljut	[loot]
Lonely	Usamljen	[OO-sah-mehl-yehn]
Tired	Umoran	[OO-maw-ran]
Thirsty	Zedan	[JAY-dahn]
Sad	Tuzan	[too-JAHN]
Happy	Sretan	[SRAY-ton]
Worried	Zabrinut	[zah-BREE-noot]
Hurt	Povrijedjen	[poh-VREE-jehm]

Commands/Requests

Be quiet.	Usuti.	[OO-shoo-TEE]
Don't run.	Ne trci.	[neh tur-CHEE]
Stop!	Stoj!	[stoi]
Line up.	Postroji se.	[poh-STROI-yee seh]

Serbo-Croatian

English	Serbo-Croatian	Pronunciation
Stand up.	Vstani.	[oo-STAH-nee]
Come here.	Dodji ovdje.	[dod-JEE aww-dah-yeh]
Point to...	Pokazati..	[POH-kah-zaz-tee]
Don't touch!	Ne diraj!	[neh DIH-ray]
I need help.	Potrebna mi je pomoc.	[POH-treb-nah mee YEH]
May I?	Da li mogu?	[DAH-LEE moh-goo]
Let's go!	Idemo!	[EE-deh-moh]
Raise your hand.	Digni ruku.	[dihg-NEE reo-koo]
Look.	Gledaj.	[glay-DAY]

Affirmations/Negations

English	Serbo-Croatian	Pronunciation
Good!	Dobro!	[daw-braw]
Great work!	Dobro uradjeno!	[daw-braw oo-rah-jay-noh]
That's better.	To je bolje.	[toh-yeh BOHL-yeh]
O.K.	O.K.	Same as English

School and Classroom Furnishings

English	Serbo-Croatian	Pronunciation
Desk	Klupa	[KLOO-pah]
Chair	Stolica	[STAW-lee-tzah]
Table	Sto	[stoh]
Chalkboard	Tabla	[TAH-blah]
Flag	Zastava	[ZAHS-ta vah]
Door	Vrata	[VRAH-tah]
Window	Prozor	[PROH-zor]
Closet	Spremnica	[SPREHM-nee-tza]
Trash can	Kanta za smece	[KAHN-tah ZA smeh-CHAY]
Hallway	Hodnik	[hod-nihk]
Office	Ured	[OO-rehd]
Boys'/Girls' Toilet	Muski zahod / Zenski zahod	[MOOSHI-kee/jen-skee, za-hohd]

English	Serbo-Croatian	Pronunciation
Gym	Voezbaonica	[VYEHZ-bah-aw NEE-tzah]
Lunchroom	Prostorija za objed	[PRAW-STAW-ree-ah zah-OB-yehd]
Pen	Pero	[PEH-roh]
Pencil	Olovka	[aw-lov-kah]
Paper	Papir	[pah-PIHR]
Tissue	Maramica	[MAH-RAH-mee-tzah]
Book	Knjiga	[K-NEE-gah]
Shelf	Polica	[PAW-LEE-tzah]

School Activities

English	Serbo-Croatian	Pronunciation
Homework	Domaci zadatak	[DOH-MAH-chee ZAH-DAH-tahk]
Test	Test	Same as English
Report	Skolska svjedodzba	[SHKOHL-skah S-VYEHD-dawj-bah]
Study	Uciti	[OO-cheh-tay]
Read	Citati	[CHEE-tah-tay]
Write	Pisati	[PEE-sah-tay]
Draw	Crtati	[SEHR-tah-tay]
Listen	Slusati	[SLOO-shah-tay]
Take this home to your parents.	Ponesi to doma roditeljima.	[POH-neh-see TOH DOH-mah roh-deh-tehl-yee-mah]

Spanish

English	Translation	Pronunciation
People		
I	Yo	[yoh]
Me	Mí	[mih]
You	Tú	[too]
You (plural)	Ustedes	[ooz-TED-ehs]
She	Ella	[EH-yah]
He	Él	[EL]
It	Él	[EL]
We	Nosotros	[noh-SOH-trohz]
Us	Nosotros	[noh-SOH-trohz]
They	Ellos	[EH-yohz]
Them	Ellos	[EH-yohz]
My name is…	Mí nombre es…	[mih NOHM-breh ehz]
Teacher	Maestra	[mah-EHS-trah]
Student	Estudiante	[ehs-too-dee-AHN-teh]
Principal	Director	[dih-rek-TOHR]
Parent	Madre, Padre	[MAH-dreh PAH-dre]
Mother	Mamá	[mah-MAH]
Father	Papá, Padre	[pah-PAH PAH-dreh]
Sister	Hermana	[air-MAH-nah]
Brother	Hermano	[air-MAH-noh]
Parts of the Body		
Face	Cara	[KAH-rah]
Eye	Ojo	[O-ho]
Nose	Naríz	[nah-REES]
Mouth	Boca	[BOH-kah]
Ear	Oreja	[oar-REH-ha]
Hand	Mano	[MAH-noh]
Finger	Dedo	[DEH-doh]
Thumb	Dedo gordo	[DEH-doh GOAR-doh]
Arm	Brazo	[BRAH-soh]
Leg	Pierna	[pee-EHR-nah]
Feet	Pie	[pee-EH]
Clothing, "body furniture"		
Hat	Sombrero	[sohm-BREH-roh]
	Gorra	[GOAR-rah]
Glove	Guante	[WAN-teh]
Eyeglasses	Gafas	[GAH-fahz]
	Anteojos	[ahn-teh-O-hos]
Wheelchair	Silla de ruedas	[SIH-ya deh roo-WEH-dahs]
Braces (teeth and leg)	Frenos	[FREH-nos]
	Refuerzos de piernas	[reh-FWEH-sos deh pee-EHR-nahz]
Crutches	Muletas	[moo-LEH-tahz]
Coat	Abrigo	[ah-BREE-goh]
Sweater	Suéter	[soo-WEH-tehr]
Shirt	Camisa	[kah-MEE-sah]
Slacks (pants)	Pantalones	[pahn-tah-LOHN-ehs]
Shoes	Zapatos	[sah-PAH-tohs]
Socks	Calcetines	[kahl-seh-TEEN-ehs]
Time		
Soon	Pronto	[PROHN-toh]

Spanish

English	Spanish	Pronunciation
Now	Ahora	[ah-OH-rah]
Later	Más tarde	[MAHZ TAHR-deh]
Today	Hoy	[oy]
This morning	Esta mañana	[EHZ-tah mah-NYAH-nah]
This afternoon	Esta tarde	[EHZ-tah TA-IR-deh]
Tonight	Esta noche	[EHZ-tah NCH-chay]
Yesterday	Ayer	[ah-YEHR]
Tomorrow	Mañana	[mah-NYAF-nah]

Place

English	Spanish	Pronunciation
Front	Delante de	[deh-LAHN-teh deh]
Back	Detrás de	[deh-TRAHZ deh]
Up	Arriba	[ahr-REE-bah]
Down	Abajo	[ah-BAH-ho]
On top	Sobre arriba	[SOH-breh ahr-REE-bah]
Underneath	Debajo	[deh-BAH-ho]
Here	Aquí	[ah-KEE]
There	Allí	[ah-YEE]
Inside	Dentro	[DEHN-troh]
	Adentro	[ah-DEHN-troh]
In	En	[ehn]
Out	Fuera	[FWEH-rah]
Left	Izquierda	[eez-KYE-IR-dah]
Right	Derecha	[deh-REH-chah]

Human Relations
Greetings, Goodbyes

English	Spanish	Pronunciation
Hello	Hola	[OH-lah]
Goodbye	Adios	[ah-DEE-ohz]
Can I help?	¿Te puedo ayudar?	[te poo-WEH-doh ah-YOO-dahr]

English	Spanish	Pronunciation
I feel sick.	No me siento bien.	[noh meh see-EHN-toh BEE-ehn]
Help me.	Ayúdame.	[ah-YOO-dah-meh]
I love you.	Te quiero.	[teh kee-YEH-roh]
Do you need to use the bathroom?	¿Necesitas usar el cuarto de baño?	[neh-seh-SEE-tahz oo-SAHR el KWAHR-toh deh BAH-nyoh]
Don't worry.	No te ocupes.	[noh teh oh-KOO-pehz]
	No te preocupes.	[noh teh preh-oh-KOO-pehz]
Can I borrow that?	¿Me prestas esto?	[meh PREHZ-tahz EHS-toh]
Excuse me.	Perdóname.	[pehr-DOHN-ah-meh]

Manners

English	Spanish	Pronunciation
Please	Por favor	[pohr fah-VOHR]
Thank you	Gracias	[GRAH-see-ahs]
Yes	Sí	[SEE]
No	No	[noh]
May I?	¿Me permites?	[meh pehr-MEE-tehz]
I'm sorry.	Lo siento.	[loh see-EHN-toh]

Feelings

English	Spanish	Pronunciation
Hungry	Tener hambre	[teh-NEHR AHM-breh]
Angry	Enojado(a)	[ehn-noh-HA-doh]
Lonely	Solo(a)	[SOH-loh]
Tired	Cansado(a)	[kan-SAH-doh]
Thirsty	Sediento, tener sed	[teh-NEHR sehd]
Sad	Triste	[TREEZ-teh]
Happy	Felíz	[feh-LEEZ]
Worried	Preocupado(a)	[preh-oh-koo-PAH-doh]
Hurt	Herido(a)	[eh-REE-doh]

Spanish

English	Spanish	Pronunciation
Trash can	Bote de basura	[BOH-teh deh bah-SOO-rah]
Hallway	Pasillo	[pah-SEE-yoh]
Office	Oficina	[oh-fee-SEE-nah]
Boys'/Girls' Toilet	Cuarto de baño de Niños/niñas	[KWAR-toh deh BAH-nyoh deh NEE-nyohs/NEE-nyahs]
Gym	Gimnasio	[heem-NAH-see-oh]
Lunchroom	Cafetería	[ka-feh-teh-REE-ah]
Pen	Pluma	[PLOO-mah]
Pencil	Lápiz	[LAH-peehz]
Paper	Papel	[pah-PEHL]
Tissue	Pañuelo de papel	[pah-NWEH-loh deh pah PEL]
Book	Libro	[LEE-broh]
Shelf	Estante	[ehs-TAHN-teh]

School Activities

English	Spanish	Pronunciation
Homework	Tarea	[tah-REH-ah]
Test	Prueba	[proo-WEH-bah]
Report	Reporte	[reh-POHR-teh]
Study	Estudio	[ehs-TOO-dee-oh]
Read	Leer	[leh-EHR]
Write	Escribir	[ehs-kree-BIHR]
Draw	Dibujar	[dee-boo-HAR]
Listen	Escuchar	[ehs-koo-CHAHR]
Take this home to your parents.	Lleven esto a casa a sus padres.	[YEH-vehn EHS-toh ah KAH-sah ah soos PAH-drehz.]

Commands/Requests

English	Spanish	Pronunciation
Be quiet.	¡Silencio!	[see-LEN-see-oh]
Don't run.	No corran.	[noh KO-rrahn]
Stop!	¡alto!	[AHL-toh]
Line up.	Pónganse en fila.	[POHN-gahn-seh ehn FEE lah]
Stand up.	Pónganse de pie.	[POHN-gahn-seh deh pee-EH]
Come here.	Ven aquí.	[vehn ah-KEE]
Point to...	Apuntar, apunten...	[ah-POOHN-tehn]
Don't touch!	!No toquen!	[no TOH-kehn]
I need help.	Necesito ayuda.	[neh-seh-SEE-toh ah-YOO dah]
May I?	¿Me permites?	[meh pehr-MEE-tehz]
Let's go!	¡Vámonos!	[VAH-moh-nohz]
Raise your hand.	Alza la mano.	[AHL sah lah MAH-noh]
Look	Mira	[MEE-rah]

Affirmations/Negations

English	Spanish	Pronunciation
Good!	Dime	[DEE-meh]
Great work!	Muy bién	[mooy bee-EHN]
That's better!	Otra vez	[OH-trah vehz]
O.K.	seguro	[seh-GOO-roh]

School and Classroom Furnishings

English	Spanish	Pronunciation
Desk	escritorio	[es-kree-TOH-ree-oh]
Chair	silla	[SEE-yah]
Table	mesa	[MEH-sah]
Chalkboard	pizarra	[pee-SAH-rra]
Flag	Bandera	[bahn-DEH-rah]
Door	Puerta	[PWER-tah]
Window	Ventana	[ven-TAHN-nah]
Closet	Guardarropa	[wahr-dah-RROH-pah]

Tagalog

English	Translation	Pronunciation
People		
I	Ako	[a-KO]
Me	Ako	[a-KO]
You	Ikaw	[i-KAW]
You (plural)	Kayo	[ka-YO]
She	Siya	[si-YA]
He	Siya	[si-YA]
It	Iyon	[i-YON]
We	Namin	[na-MIN]
Us	Kami	[ka-MI]
They	Sila	[si-LA]
Them	Nila	[ni-LA]
My name is...	Ang pangalan ko ay...	[ang pa-NGA-lan ko AY]
Teacher	Guro	[GU-ro]
Student	Magaaral	[MAG-a-a-ral]
Principal	Punong guro	[pu-NONG GU-ro]
Parent	Magulang	[ma-gu-LANG]
Mother	Ina	[i-NA]
Father	Ama	[a-MA]
Sister	Kapatid na babae	[ka-pa-TID na ba-ba-E]
Brother	Kapatid na lalaki	[ka-pa-TID na la-la-KI]
Parts of the Body		
Face	Mukha	[MUK-ha]
Eye	Mata	[MA-ta]
Nose	Ilong	[i-LONG]
Mouth	Bibig	[bi-BIG]
Ear	Taenga	[ta-e-NGA]
Hand	Kamay	[ka-MAY]
Finger	Daliri	[da-li-RI]
Thumb	Hinlalaki	[HIN-la-la-KI]
Arm	Braso	[bra-SO]
Leg	Binti	[bin-TI]
Feet	Paa	[pa-A]
Clothing, "body furniture"		
Hat	Sambalilo	[sam-ba-LI-lo]
Glove	Guwantes	[gu-WAN-tes]
Eyeglasses	Salamin sa mata	[sa-la-MIN sa ma-TA]
wheelchair	Upuan na maygulong	[u-PU-an na may-gu-LONG]
Braces (teeth and leg)	Benda sa binti	[ben-DA sa bin-TI]
Crutches	Saklay	[SAK-lay]
Coat	Damit panglamig	[da-MIT pang-la-MIG]
Sweater	Damit panglamig	[da-MIT pang-la-MIG]
Shirt	Kamiseta	[ka-MI-se-ta]
Slacks (pants)	Pantalon	[pan-ta-LON]
Shoes	Sapatos	[sa-pa-TOS]
Socks	Mediyas	[cha-rAP-EH]
Time		
Soon	Ngayon din	[nga-YON DIN]
Now	Ngayon	[nga-YON]
later	Mamaya	[ma-ma-YA]
Today	Ngayong araw	[nga-YONG a-raw]
This morning	Popodne	[nga-YONG U-ma-ga]
This afternoon	Ngayong hapon	[nga-YONG ha-PON]

English	Tagalog	Pronunciation
Tonight	Mamayang gabi	[ma-ma-YANG ga-BI]
Yesterday	Akahapon	[ka-ha-PON]
Tomorrow	Bukas	[bu-KAS]

Place

English	Tagalog	Pronunciation
Front	Harapan	[ha-ra-PAN]
Back	Likuran	[li-ku-RAN]
Up	Itaas	[i-ta-AS]
Down	Ibaba	[i-ba-BA]
On top	Sa taas	[sa-ta-AS]
Underneath	Sa ilalim	[sa i-la-LIM]
Here	Dito	[DI-to]
There	Doon	[do-on]
Inside	Sa loob	[sa lo-ob]
In	Pasok	[pa-SOK]
Out	Labas	[la-BAS]
Left	Kaliwa	[ka-LI-wa]
Right	Kanan	[ka-NAN]

Human Relations
Greetings, Goodbyes

English	Tagalog	Pronunciation
Hello	Kumusta	[ku-MUS-ta]
Goodbye	Paalam	[pa-a-LAM]
Can I help?	Puwede bang makatulongg?	[pu-we-de BANG ma-ka-tu-LONG]
I feel sick.	M asama ang ak-ing pakiramdam.	[ma-sa-ma ang a KING pa-KI-ram-dam]
Help me.	tulungan ako.	[tu-lu-NGAN a-ko]
I love you.	mahal kita.	[ma-hal KI-ta]
Do you need to use the bathroom?	Kailangan mo bang Gamitin ang pali kuran?	[ka-I-la-ngan mo BANG ga-mi-TIN ang pa-LI ku- ran]

English	Tagalog	Pronunciation
Don't worry.	Huwag magalala.	[hu-wag MAG-a-la-la]
Can I borrow that?	Puwede bang mah Iram i yan?	[pu-we-de BANG ma-hi-RAM I-yan]
Excuse me.	Makikiraan.	[ma-KI-KI-ra-an]

Manners

English	Tagalog	Pronunciation
Please	Puwede ba	[pu-we-de BA]
Thank you	Salamat	[sa-la-MAT]
Yes	O,o	[oh-oh]
No	Hindi	[hin-DI]
May I?	Maaari ba?	[ma-a-ri BA]
I'm sorry.	Ipagpaumanhi mo.	[I-pag-pa-u-man-HI-mo]

Feelings

English	Tagalog	Pronunciation
Hungry	Gutom	[gu-TOM]
Angry	Galit	[ga-LIT]
Lonely	Nalulungkot	[na-lu-LUNG-kot]
Tired	Pagod	[pa-GOD]
Thirsty	Uhaw	[u-HAW]
Sad	Malungkot	[ma-LUNG-kot]
Happy	Masaya	[ma-sa-ya]
Worried	Nag aalala	[NAG a-a-la-la]
Hurt	Nasaktan	[na-SAK-tan]

Commands/Requests

English	Tagalog	Pronunciation
Be quiet.	Huwag magingay.	[HU-wag mag-I-ngay]
Don't run.	Huwag tumakbo.	[HU-wag tu-MAK-bo]
Stop!	Hinto!	[HIN-to]
Line up.	Pumila sa linya.	[PU-mi-la sa LIN-yan]
Stand up.	Tumayo.	[TU-na-yo]
Come here.	Halika rito.	[ha-LI-ka RI-to]

Point to...	Ituro	[i-TU-ro]
Don't touch!	Huwag hawakan!	[HU-wag ha-WA-kan]
I need help.	Kailangan ko ang tulong.	[ka-I-la-ngan ko ang tu-LONG]
May I?	Puwede ba?	[pu-WE-de BA]
Let's go!	Halika na!	[ha-li-KA na]
Look	Tumingin	[tu-mi-NGIN]

Affirmations/Negations

Good!	Magaling!	[maga-LING]
Great work!	Magaling na trabaho!	[maga-LING na tra-ba-HO]
That's better!	Magaling mo uli!	[ga-wa-IN mo u-LI]
O.K.	Okay	[O-kay]

School and Classroom Furnishings

Desk	Mesang sulutan	[me-SANG su-la-tan]
Chair	Upuan	[u-PU-an]
Table	Mesa	[me-sa]
Chalkboard	Pisara	[PI-sa-ra]
Flag	Bandila	[ban-DI-la]
Front	Harapan	[ha-ra-PAN]
Back	Likuran	[li-KU-ran]
Door	Pintuan	[pin-TU-an]
Window	Bintana	[BIN-ta-na]
Closet	Aparador	[spremnitza]
Trash can	Basurahan	[ba-SU-ra-han]
Hallway	Daanan ng tad	[da-a-nan NG ta-O]
Office	Opisina	[o-pi-SI-na]
Boys'/Girls' Toilet	Lalaki palikuran / Babae palikuran	[la-la-KI pa-li-KU-ran] / [ba-ba-E pa-li-KU-ran]
Gym	Lugar para sa pag-hehersisyo	[LU-gar pa-ra sa pag-he-her-SIS-yo]

Lunchroom	Kantina	[kan-TI-na]
Pen	Pluma	[PLU-ma]
Pencil	Lapis	[la-PIS]
Paper	Papel	[pa-pel]
Tissue	Papel sa palikuran	[pa-pel sa pa-li-KU-ran]
Book	Libro	[LIB-ro]
Shelf	Lalagyan ng libro	[la-lag-yan ng LI-bro]

School Activities

Homework	Takdang aralin	[TAK-dang ara-LIN]
Test	Pagsusulit	[pag-su-su-LIT]
Report	Mark a sa pag susulit	[mar-ka sa-pag-su-su-LIT]
Study	Magaral	[MAG-a-ral]
Read	Magbasa	[MAG-ba-sa]
Write	Magsulat	[MAG-su-lat]
Draw	Magdrawing	[MAG-dra-wing]
Listen	Makinig	[ma-KI-nig]
Take this home to your parents.	Dalhin sa bahay at ipakita sa mag-ulang.	[dal-HIN sa ba-dohma RODE-it-hay at i-pa-KI-ta sa ma-GU-lang]

Urdu

English	Translation	Pronunciation
People		
I	مَیں	[mayn]
Me	مجھے	[moo-JAY]
You	تُم	[toom]
You (plural)	تُم	[toom]
She	وہ	[voh]
He	وہ	[voh]
It	یہ	[yay]
We	ہم	[hum]
Us	ہمیں	[huh-MAYN]
They	وہ	[voh]
Them	اُنہیں	[oon-HAYN]
My name is...	میرا نام ہے --	[meh-RAH nahm-HAY]
Teacher	اُستاد	[OOS-tahd]
Student	طالب علم	[tah-LEE-BAY ihlm]
Principal	پرنسپل	Same as English
Parent	والدین	[WAA-li-dain]
Mother	ماں ، والدہ	[mahn, VAHL-dah]
Father	باپ ، والد	[bahp, vah-LIHD]
Sister	بہن	[beh-HEHN]
Brother	بھائی	[bhai]
Parts of the Body		
Face	چہرہ	[CHEH-rah]
Eye	آنکھ	[ahn-KAYN]
Nose	ناک	[nahk]

English	Translation	Pronunciation
Mouth	مُنہ	[moon]
Ear	کان	[kahn]
Hand	ہاتھ	[haht]
Finger	اُنگلی	[OONG-lee-ahn]
Thumb	اَنگوٹھا	[ahn-GOO-tah]
Arm	ہاتھ	[haht]
Leg	ٹانگ	[tah-AHNG]
Feet	پاوں	[pah-ON]
Clothing, "body furniture"		
Hat	ٹوپی	[toh-PEE]
Glove	دستانہ	[dus-TAH-NAY]
Eyeglasses	چشمہ	[CHAWSH-mah]
Wheelchair	پہیے والی کرسی	[PAY-yeh wah-LEE kur-SEE]
Braces (teeth and leg)	دانتوں کی تاریں	[Daanto'n ki Taarai'n]
Crutches	بیساکھیاں کلرچیاں	[beh-sah-KEE]
Coat	کوٹ	Same as English
Sweater	سویٹر	Same as English
Shirt	قمیض	[kah-MEEZ]
Slacks (pants)	پتلون	[pat-LOON]
Shoes	جوتے	[joo-tay]
Socks	موزے	[moh-zay]
Time		
Soon	جلدی	[jahl-DEE]
Now	اب	[ub]
Later	بعد میں	[bahd-MAYN]
Today	آج	[ahj]
This morning	آج صبح	[ahj soo-bah]
This afternoon	آج سہ پہر	[AHJ-seh peh-HEHR]
Tonight	آج رات	[ahj raht]

English	Urdu	Pronunciation
Yesterday	گزشتہ کل	[goo-zihsh-TAH KULL]
Tomorrow	کل	[kull]
Place		
Front	سامنے	[sahm-NAY]
Back	پیچھے	[pee-CHAY]
Up	اوپر	[OO-purr]
Down	نیچے	[nee-CHAY]
On top	کے اوپر	[KAY OO-purr]
Underneath	نیچے	[nee-CHAY]
Here	یہاں	[yah-HAHN]
There	وہاں	[wah-HAHN]
Inside	اندر	[un-DAHR]
In	میں	[mayn]
Out	باہر	[bah-HAR-kah-RIHJ]
Left	بائیں	[BAH-yan-OOL-tah]
Right	دائیں	[DAH-yan-SEE-dah]
Human Relations		
Greetings, Goodbyes		
Hello	السلام علیکم	[ah-sah-LAHM oo wah-LAY-kum]
Goodbye	خدا حافظ	[KOO-dah hah-fehz]
Can I help?	کیا میں مدد کر سکتا ہوں	[kyah MAYN mah-DAHD cur SAHK-tah HOON]
I feel sick.	میں بیمار ہوں	[MEHN bee-MAHR HOON]
Help me.	میری مدد کریں	[may-REE mah-DAHD kah-RAYN]
I love you.	میں آپ سے محبت کرتا ہوں	[moo-JAY ahp SAY]
Do you need to use the bathroom?	کیا آپ کو غسل خانہ استعمال کرنا ہے	[Keeya aap nai'n Gussal Khena Isammaal Karna Hai]

English	Urdu	Pronunciation
Don't worry.	فکر نہ کریں	[fih-KAHR NAH kah-RAYN]
Can I borrow that?	کیا میں یہ ادھار لے سکتا ہوں	[kyah MAYN woh oo-DAHR LAY sahk-tah HOON]
Excuse me.	معاف کیجیے	[mahf kee-jee-AY]
Manners		
Please	براہِ مہربانی	[ba-rah-AY, meh-HEHR-bah]
Thank you	شکریہ	[shook-REE-ah]
Yes	جی	[jee]
No	نہیں	[nah-HEEN]
May I?	کیا مجھے اجازت ہے	[KYAH moo-JAY eh-JAH-zaht HAY]
I'm sorry	مجھے افسوس ہے	[moo-JAY ahf-sos HAY]
Feelings		
Hungry	بھوکا	[bhoo-KAH]
Angry	غصے میں	[ghoo-say MEHN]
Lonely	تنہا	[tun-HAH]
Tired	تھکا ہوا	[tah-KAH HOO-ah]
Thirsty	پیاسا	[PYAH-sah]
Sad	اداس	[run-JEE-dah]
Happy	خوش	[khoish]
Worried	پریشان	[pree-SHAN]
Hurt	دکھا ہوا	[doo-KAH hoo-AH]
Commands/Requests		
Be quiet.	خاموش ہو جاؤ	[kah-MOSH hoh-JAO]
Don't run.	دوڑو مت	[bah-GOH MUTT]
Stop!	رک جاؤ	[rook JAO]
Line up.	لائن بناؤ	[LYNE bah-NAO]
Stand up.	کھڑے ہو جاؤ	[kah-RAY hoh-JAO]

English	Urdu	Pronunciation
Come here.	یہاں آؤ	[yah-HAHN ah-oh]
Point to...	اشارہ کرو	[IH-shah-rah ka-ROH]
Don't touch!	مت چھوؤ	[MUTT CHOO-oh]
I need help.	مجھے مدد چاہیے	[moo-JAY mah-DAHD chah-ee-ay]
May I?	کیا اجازت ہے	[moo-JAY ee-JAH-zaht HAY]
Let's go!	چلو چلیں	[chah-LOH CHAH-lehn]
Raise your hand.	اپنا ہاتھ کھڑا کرو	[UP-nah haht KAH-rah kah-ROH]
Look	دیکھو	[day-KOH]

Affirmations/Negations

English	Urdu	Pronunciation
Good!	شاباش	[shah-bahsh]
Great work!	زبردست کام	[zah-BAHR-dust KAHU]
That's better!	یہ بہتر ہے	[yeh beh-TAHR HAY]
O.K.	ٹھیک ہے	[teek HAY]

School and Classroom Furnishings

English	Urdu	Pronunciation
Desk	میز	[mayz]
Chair	کرسی	[koor-SEE]
Table	میز	[mayz]
Chalkboard	تختۂ سیاہ	Same as English
Flag	جھنڈا	[jahn-dah]
Door	دروازہ	[der-wah-ZAH]
Window	کھڑکی	[kayr-KEE]
Closet	الماری	[ahl-mah-REE]
Trash can	کوڑے کا ڈبہ	[koo-RAy kah dub-BAH]
Hallway	ہال	Same as English
Office	دفتر	[daf-dahr]
Boys'/Girls' Toilet	مردانہ/زنانہ ٹوائلٹ	[ZAH-nah-nah toilet]
Lunchroom	کھانے کا کمرہ	[kah-NAY kah kam-RAH]

English	Urdu	Pronunciation
Pen	قلم	Same as English
Pencil	پنسل	Same an English
Paper	کاغذ	[kah-Guz]
Tissue	ٹشو	Same as English
Book	کتابیں	[kee-TAH-bayn]
Shelf	تختے	[TAHK-tay]

School Activities

English	Urdu	Pronunciation
Homework	گھر کے لیے کام	[gahr KAY lee-AY kam]
Test	امتحان	[IM-teh-hhahn]
Report	رپورٹ	[kah-GUZ]
Study	مطالعہ	[moh-tah-LAY-yah]
Read	پڑھو	[pah-ROH]
Write	لکھو	[lihk-KOH]
Draw	بناؤ/چیزیں	[bah-NAO]
Listen	سنو	[soo-NOH]
Take this home to your parents.	یہ اپنے والدین کے گھر لے جاؤ	[YEH up-NAY wahl-DAYN KAY]

Vietnamese

English	Translation	Pronunciation
People		
I	Tôi	[doi]
Me	Tôi	[doi]
You	Anh/Chị	[ahn/jay]
You (plural)	Các anh/Các chị	[GACK ahn/gack jay]
She	Chị/Cô/Bà	[jay/goh/bah]
He	Anh/Ông ấy	[ahn/ong AHEE]
It	Nó/Cái đó	[naw/gye daw]
We	Chúng tôi	[JOONG - doi]
Us	Chúng tôi	[JOONG - doi]
They	Họ	[haw]
Them	Họ	[haw]
My name is...	Tôi tên là...	[doi dihn LAH]
Teacher	Thầy giáo	[tye ZAO]
Student	Học sinh	[hawk sihn]
Principal	Hiệu trưởng	[hyoo chœong]
Parent	Cha mẹ	[JAH may]
Mother	Mẹ	[meh]
Father	Cha	[jah]
Sister	Chị/Em	[jay/ehm]
Brother	Anh/Em	[ahn/ehm]
Parts of the Body		
Face	Mặt	[maht]
Eye	Mắt	[maht]
Nose	Mũi	[MOO-ee]
Mouth	Miệng	[MEE-eng]
Ear	Tai	[dye]
Hand	Tay	[dye]
Finger	Ngón tay	[hnon DYE]
Thumb	Ngón cái	[hnon GYE]
Arm	Cánh tay	[gahn dye]
Leg	Chân	[jahn]
Feet	Bàn chân	[bahn JAHN]
Clothing, "body furniture"		
Hat	Nón	[non]
Glove	Bao tay	[bao DYE]
Eyeglasses	Mắt kiếng	[MAHT kee-ehm]
Wheelchair	Xe lăn	[shay LAHN]
Braces (teeth and leg)	Niềng răng / Dây đeo quần	[nee-ehng RAHNG / zye day-oh GWAHN]
Crutches	Nạng	[nahng]
Coat	Áo khoác	[ao kwock]
Sweater	Áo lạnh	[ao lahn]
Shirt	Áo sơ mi	[ao sih MEE]
Slacks (pants)	Quần	[gwahn]
Shoes	Giày	[zah-ee]
Socks	Vớ	[vaw]
Time		
Soon	Sắp sửa	[sop sih-ah]
Now	Bây giờ	[bye ZAH]
Later	Sau này	[sow NYE]
Today	Hôm nay	[hom NYE]
This morning	Sáng nay	[sahng NYE]
This afternoon	Chiều nay	[joo NYE]

English	Vietnamese	Pronunciation
Tonight	Tối nay	[doi NYE]
Yesterday	Hôm qua	[hom KWA]
Tomorrow	Ngày mai	[hnye MYE]

Place

English	Vietnamese	Pronunciation
Front	Phía trước	[fiah CHOO-AWK]
Back	Phía sau	[fiah SOW]
Up	Lên	[lehn]
Down	Xuống	[shoo-awn]
On top	Ở trên	[aw chehn]
Underneath	Ở dưới	[aw zoh-ee]
Here	Ở đây	[aw dye]
There	Kia	[geh-ih]
Inside	Trong	[chawng]
In	Vô	[voh]
Out	Ra	[rah]
Left	Trái	[CHAH-ih]
Right	Phải	[FAH-ih]

Human Relations
Greetings, Goodbyes

English	Vietnamese	Pronunciation
Hello	Mạnh giỏi	[mahn YOI]
Goodbye	Tạm biệt	[dahm BEE-eht]
Can I help?	Cần gì không	[gahn zee KAWNG]
I feel sick.	Tôi không khỏe	[doi KONG kway]
Help me.	Xin giúp tôi	[sihn JOOP doi]
I love you.	Tôi thương em	[doi toong ehm]
Do you need to use the bathroom?	Có cần phòng tắm không?	[goh kahn FAHNG tahm KAHNG]
Don't worry.	Đừng lo	[doong LAW]

English	Vietnamese	Pronunciation
Can I borrow that?	Tôi có thể mượn không?	[DOI goh tay moon kahng]
Excuse me.	Xin lỗi	[sihn LOI]

Manners

English	Vietnamese	Pronunciation
Please	Làm ơn	[lahm AWN]
Thank you	Cám ơn	[gahm awn]
Yes	Vâng	[vehng]
No	Không	[kawng]
May I?	Xin phép	[sihn fehp]
I'm sorry	Xin lỗi	[sihn loi]

Feelings

English	Vietnamese	Pronunciation
Hungry	Đói	[doi]
Angry	Giận	[yahn]
Lonely	Cô đơn	[goh dawn]
Tired	Mệt	[meht]
Thirsty	Khát	[kaht]
Sad	Buồn	[boo-AWN]
Happy	Vui	[voo-i]
Worried	Lo âu	[law AU]
Hurt	Đau khổ	[DAO koh]

Commands/Requests

English	Vietnamese	Pronunciation
Be quiet.	Im	[ihm]
Don't run.	Đừng chạy	[doong JYE]
Stop!	Đứng lại!	[doong LYE]
Line up.	Sắp hàng	[SAHP hang]
Stand up.	Đứng dậy	[doong ZYE]
Come here.	Tới đây.	[doi DYE]

Pen	Viết	[VEE-eht]
Pencil	Viết chì	[VEE-eht JAY]
Paper	Giấy	[zye]
Tissue	Khăn	[kahn]
Book	Sách	[sahk]
Shelf	Kệ	[geh]

School Activities

Homework	Bài làm	[bye lahm]
Test	Thi	[tee]
Report	Học bạ	[hawk BAH]
Study	Học	[hawk]
Read	Đọc	[dawk]
Write	Viết	[VEE - eht]
Draw	Vẽ	[veh]
Listen	Nghe	[hneh]
Take this home to your parents.	Đem về đưa cha mẹ	[dehm VAY doo BOH meh]

Point to...	Chỉ vào...	[JAY vaw]
Don't touch!	Đừng đụng	[doong doong]
I need help.	Xin giúp tôi	[sihn JOOP doi]
May I?	Xin phép	[sihn fehp]
Are you...?	Kya tum?	[kya-tum]
Let's go!	Đi thôi	[day toi]
Raise your hand.	Đưa tay lên	[DOO dye lehn]
Look.	Coi kìa	[goi ga]

Affirmations/Negations

Good!	Tốt lắm	[DAWT lam]
Great work!	Giỏi	[yoi]
That's better!	Khá hơn	[KAH hoon]
O.K.	O.K. - Đồng ý	[DAWNG ay]

School and Classroom Furnishings

Desk	Bàn học	[bahn hawk]
Chair	Ghế	[gay]
Table	Bàn	[bahn]
Chalkboard	Bảng đen	[bahn DEHN]
Flag	Cờ	[goh]
Door	Cửa	[gih]
Window	Cửa sổ	[gih SHAW]
Closet	Tủ	[doh]
Trash can	Thùng rác	[toong RAK]
Hallway	Hành lang	[hahn LANG]
Office	Văn phòng	[vahn FAWNG]
Boys'/Girls' Toilet	Phòng tắm nam	[FAWNG dahm nahm]
	Phòng tắm nữ	[fawng dahm NOO]
Gym	Phòng tập	[fawng tahp]
Lunchroom	Phòng ăn	[fawng AEN]